FINDING YOUR
YOUR
WOOOOOO!

Charleston, SC
www.PalmettoPublishing.com

FINDING YOUR WOOOOO!
Copyright © 2021 by Chad Cannon

First Edition

Paperback ISBN: 978-1-68515-549-0
eBook ISBN: 978-1-68515-550-6

HEALTH & FITNESS SUCCESS STRATEGIES

FINDING YOUR

WOOOOO!

CHAD CANNON

"Chad made it very easy for me to be serious about my fitness. He's a motivator, educator and sincere individual. Chad has made an enormous difference in my life, body and soul"

~ *Tamera Bream, President, Equity Payment, Inc*

"Chad's enthusiasm for health and fitness in contagious. He doesn't just focus on exercise, but genuinely engages me on my physical, mental, and spiritual well- being. While not always being the perfect client over the last four years, he has greeted me with a smile and positive attitude when I enter the gym. He holds me accountable for my personal health and well-being."

~ *James Atkins, President, Architect of Court Atkins Group*

"I met Chad as my Cross-Country Coach in high school. Chad has helped me become a stronger athlete, not only physically but mentally as well. The time I spent training with Chad, he has told me to carry a "Champion Mindset". This has been my main motto as I'm taking on my last year as a student athlete in high school. This is something I will forever carry on through my future athletic career and in life. The more time I spend training with Chad I feel an improvement with the mental game of the sport. I feel stronger and mentally prepared more than ever before! Thanks to Chad, he has taught me to be confident with my body when it comes to performance. I am always grateful for all the things Chad has taught me as an athlete and as a person."

~ *Victoria Sosa, Student Athlete at May River High School*

"Chad has helped me become the best soccer player I can be. He has done so much for me for my journey to become a pro soccer. Without him, I wouldn't be as prepared and ready for challenges as I am today. All I can say is thank you for everything."

~ *Uriel Zarracan, Student/Athlete at Newberry College*

I started coming to Chad about 90 days after I completed physical therapy for a pretty major back surgery. I had 3 of my lumbar discs replaced with prosthetics. Prior to this I lived with back pain for close to 6 years. When I arrived to see Chad I was well on my way to mending physically, but mentally I had a long way to go to give myself permission to push the capabilities of my body. Chad and I have been working together for a few months now and the difference is huge. Physically I'm doing things I haven't done in years. For me though the most important part is the mental strength I now have to trust my body again. Thank you so much Chad for helping me get my life back!!!

~ *Andy Richard, Commercial Relationship Manager, South Atlantic Bank*

Before joining CannonFit I was working out 4-5 days a week with little results. Now I'm working out fewer days and have seen great results. Chad tailors each work out to fit your needs and keeps it different each week! He encourages you along the way. CannonFit has made me enjoy working out! I look forward to it each week!

~ *Molly Barrs, Interior designer, Shoreline Construction*

"I have always been active, but I had been looking for a way to gain strength and take my workouts to a higher level. A friend introduced me to Chad and right away I knew I had found what I was looking for. Chad pushed my limits and showed me what I was capable of. He also taught me how to fuel my body, in a way that was easy for me. I travel full-time for a living and I have easily been able to incorporate what Chad has taught me even when flying all over the place. Chad knows his stuff and I feel very lucky to have found him."

~ Lisa Archibald, First Officer for major airline

Having known Chad for 15 years, It should have made me aware much sooner than 3 ½ years ago of the reason I needed Chad in my life! I am thrilled that at least 3 ½ years ago I came to my senses and walked into his workout center. Upon my evaluation with Chad, he developed an initial workout plan and some healthy habits added in. Prior to this I had worked out for 15 years and unfortunately eased up on myself for two years and was not as strong or in shape when I hit the front door. Throughout my time with Chad, I have gained endurance, momentum, and a lifestyle balance. His patience with me as I was gaining that momentum was incredible, as I can be difficult sometime. He also was conscious of my areas of weakness like my knees, elbow and most recently my feet. His personality is so even keeled and upbeat and works so well with all the personalities that are his clients. He works closely and safely with those with Parkinson, heart issues, breathing issues, bone, and muscular degenerative issues, etc. He looks at health as a total package. He promotes not just a strong body, but a great, safe, and productive well-being. His goals are for a complete lifestyle including food, physicality, and Powerful Mindset. I love being in Chad's presence as his temperament creates such an awesome environment. Thank you, Chad, I am back to believing in myself and who I can continue to be.... strong, determined, and grateful."

~ Sandy Benson, President of Custom Audio Video

CONTENTS

FOREWORD

"DO YOU FEEL STUCK YOUR WORKOUT ROUTINE? ARE YOU GOING through the same motions every time you go to the gym and not surprisingly, seeing limited results? What if you could spend less time each day but work out with a different intensity?"

Those were the words in an article written by Chad Cannon that motivated me to reach out to him. That was five years and hundreds of workout sessions ago.

What did I find? That I *could* change up my pattern, challenge myself, and become stronger.

By nature, I am driven, disciplined and fit. I already had a workout routine. However, it had become just that – routine. With Chad's encouragement, I found that I could be better, stronger, and more focused.

Not only did we set up a more productive, time intensive program through hurricanes, pandemics, graduations, and surgeries, we conversed about life during our twice weekly sessions. We spoke about our businesses, nutrition, workout wear, the NFL, family, travel and more.

No matter age or personal fitness goals, all of us owe it to ourselves – and to our families – to seek health and well-being.

Chad guides his clients to set attainable, more manageable benchmarks, which might even mean lowering a weight-loss goal or shortening the amount of time at the gym. Why not tackle life in

1

small bites and recognize results, rather than face constant setbacks or injuries? With each milestone and advancement, small victories contribute to the whole.

Look at your day as a series of individual opportunities to make a healthy choice, instead of an "all or nothing" mentality where one slip up can derail you.

It's not hard to recognize that Chad believes in what he teaches and lives what he preaches. He structures his day, religiously follows his personal workout regimen, devotes time to family, all the while motivating and inspiring his clients.

Is it time for a change in your life? Step up your game, adjust your mindset, invest in yourself.

Turn the page, take action.

~ *Karen Moraghan, President of Hunter Public Relations*

INTRODUCTION

I WANTED TO WRITE THIS BOOK FOR PEOPLE WHO FEEL LIKE THEY need help and want to step up their game. Also for people who just want to be inspired to make changes in their mindset so they may have the ability to achieve things they think only the lucky can achieve. Everyone has the ability to succeed at whatever they want, but usually don't come close to seeing success. Not because of lack of trying, but because they simply don't know how. I've been very fortunate in having success in many areas of my life. Not lucky in that I lucked out and everything has been handed to me, because that is certainly not the case. But lucky in how I've been taught, and lucky because I have been inspired to learn more on how to grow as a person and have more success. I have reached out to so many successful people to learn from what they have done themselves. I've spoken with highly successful business people, political people, professional athletes, college athletes, high school athletes, coaches at all levels, teachers, professors, writers, speakers and many more. Any chance I get to speak to someone I know has had success I try to meet and connect with them.

I have made time to read more books, listen to podcasts, have watched thousands of videos, attended numerous seminars, and so much more. I've learned that for me to grow as a person and get my mindset in the best place possible for me to be successful in many areas of my life, its on me and me alone. So I've spent a lot of time to take in as much knowledge as I possibly can each and every day. It's an ongoing process. I never thought I would be a book reader, but I love to get my hands on a good book any chance I get. I have a thirst for learning more. I'm sure anyone that knew me during my school days would be shocked by that. As I gain more knowledge myself, I now feel the need to help others learn what I've learned. I have a passion for helping people. I always have. I'm not sure how that came to be. My guess is that I had a lot of people pour into me when I was growing up so now I want to pay it back. When I say that there were a lot that poured more into me as a youngster, I really mean it. I had a lot of great coaches who I also consider mentors, which I will mention throughout this book. Teachers, college professors, and others that I worked with who don't even know how much they taught me. I was very fortunate to have people like them in my life to teach me the ways of the world, how to have success and how failure isn't such a bad thing, how to do things like have better time management or how to form goals and vision, as well as how not to do those things. I have been wanting to write a book for many years. In fact, I started a book over twenty years ago and never finished it. I didn't finish it because I didn't have the knowledge and work ethic to know how to plan to complete it. I obviously was not ready to be any kind of author at that time in my life. Even though I had a great message to convey, it just wasn't my time to do so. Today however, I know how to plan my time, how to structure my days to complete something like this. These are the kind of things I was taught, and I want to teach you.

As a health and fitness professional over the past thirty years I have learned a lot through having had many successes and many failures. I am grateful for all of them because I would not be the man I am today had I not gone through all the good and bad times. I cannot wait for you to read what I have poured into this book, into YOU, and help give solutions so you can start having success in your body, your business, your family and in your life.

This isn't just a learn how to lose weight kind of book, or a learn how to get as fit as possible kind of book. This is more of a strategy kind of book to help you get focused in order to achieve great things in your entire life, including your health and fitness. If you follow the simple strategies I have played out for you, I know without a doubt that your life will be better. But, there is always a but, if you don't put these simple strategies to work, then you will stay the same as you are now, or even worse, become more down on yourself because you didn't do anything. So, I urge you to not just read this book, but also take notes. In fact, let's keep this simple and just **write down in your notes everything I have in bold print.** If you do that I can pretty much guarantee you'll remember what they stand for, then all you have to do is follow these super simple strategies and become more of a successful person than you will ever know. Let's Go!

Wait, before I get started I have one more thing and it's a doozy! Read this and read it well... THE THING I'M ABOUT TO SAY NEXT IS THE MOST IMPORTANT THING FOR YOU TO BE SUCCESSFUL!

I want you to imagine your life as it is right now. The things you do, the habits you have in the morning, during the day, and at night before you go to bed. Habits that have to do with your health, like eating and exercise, work habits, any self growth habits, or how much time you spend with your family and spouse. Those are habits as well. Don't forget any educational habits, relaxation habits and sleep habits. Just imagine your life, on average, as it is right now day in and day out.

Now imagine what your life would be like *one* year from now if you DIDN'T change anything and continued doing what you do now. How would you feel about yourself? How would you look? How would you perform at home, at work, at play? How would your health be? How are your relationships with your kids, spouse and friends? How would your friends and family see you in all of those things?

What about *three* years from now if you DIDN'T change anything and continued doing what you do now? How would you feel about yourself? How would you look? How would you perform at home, at work, at play? How would your health be? How are your relationships with your kids, spouse and friends? How would your friends and family see you in all of those things?

What about *five* years from now? Or *ten*, even *twenty* years? You get the point. Most likely noting would change. Or things might be worse than they currently are. Close your eyes for a second and imagine that.

Now imagine if you made some simple changes, added some simple strategies that I will go over in this book so you can have success in all parts of your life. How would you feel about yourself *one* year from now? How would you look? How would you perform at home, at work, at play? How is your health and relationships with your kids, spouse and friends? How would your friends and family see you in all of those things?

What about *three* years, *five, ten* or *twenty* years from now if you started some simple strategies to grow into success? How would you feel about yourself? How would you look? How would you perform at home, at work, at play? How would your health be? How are your relationships with your kids, spouse and friends? How would your friends and family see you in all of those things? I want you to actually close your eyes for a few seconds and imagine that? Can you see it?

I learned this technique years ago from a good friend and mentor of mine, Shane Doll. Shane, the founder of Shaping Concepts, a personal training company in Mount Pleasant, South Carolina, helped me get my brick and mortar personal training studio up and running and I owe him my life for that. If Shane didn't seek me out as a young fitness professional I wouldn't be anywhere close to where I am today. He is truly someone that has changed my life. Thank you Shane!

Here's the thing, if you get emotional about your life, I mean if you really closed yours eyes and imagined your life the way I said, and felt some kind of emotion about it, maybe even shed a tear or two, then and only then are you truly ready to make a change. If you didn't get that emotion out, try again and don't move onto Chapter 1 until you do so. If you're ready, Let's Go!

CHAPTER 1

WHERE DO YOU WANT TO BE?

'M GOING TO BE HONEST WITH YOU. I DON'T HAVE ALL THE ANSWERS. However, in this book I'm going to give you what I have learned over the years to guide you in the right direction to take you where you want to be. To achieve not just success, but major success in many different areas of your life so your fitness and health goals can easily be accomplished. I'll give you tips, strategies, helpful hints and more. Many people wanted me to write a fitness or weight loss book since I own a fitness studio and coach people. This, however is more of an overall success book. When I say overall, I mean everything from the mental aspect of having success, to making a plan for becoming successful, and of course actually doing what it takes to get there. This book will give you different ways to think about things and to go about things on a daily basis to help you become successful in your body, in your business, family, and in your everyday life. If those things are more successful after you read this book, then I know that when it comes to your health and fitness, your goals will have easily been met. After reading this book my goal for you is to wake up and yell "WOOOOO!" Workout and yell out "WOOOOO!" Go outside and yell "WOOOOO!" Achieve a daily WIN and yell out

"WOOOOO!" Meet your daily, weekly, monthly and overall goals and yell out "WOOOOO!" I want you to feel exhilarated! You know, it's that feeling you get when you accomplish something really cool, or really big and you just want to yell something out. Well, I want you to yell "WOOOOO!"

I have been truly blessed over the years. Many people might look at me and my life and say "why do you think your life is blessed?". I'm going to tell you why...

First, I have a great family! My wife Tracey and I have been married for 20 years. I love her more than she knows and she helps me become better everyday. Our marriage hasn't been easy as no marriage is, but we are still here together and each day that passes is another day of learning from each other and growing together. Tracey is and always will be my life.

We have three awesome kids; Madeline who as I write this is a senior in high school and is headed to Anderson University in upstate South Carolina next fall on a dance scholarship. She plans on double majoring in dance and exercise physiology, which I like because my degree is in exercise physiology. By the way, if you ever get to see my daughter perform a tap routine, you might be floored. My jaw drops every time I see her perform. She's truly something special! And I'm not just saying that because she's my daughter. She really is awesome!

My older of two sons, Calem, is what I call a chip off the old block. He's a lot like me. He loves sports and is really good at them. He's now a seventh grader and plays basketball for the middle school team and the high school JV team. He has also played football, and started running 5K's with me when he was much younger and runs cross country to stay in shape for basketball. His goal is to be a pro basketball player and I will encourage him as much as I possibly can instead of telling him only a few make it that far. He already knows that. He's a lot smarter than I was at his age. He gets that from his mother.

Our third child, Emerson, is our 8-year-old. He is super smart, sings every minute of the day, and is pretty good too, wants to be just like his older brother, and truly loves his parents!

We live in a beautiful house looking outside at a pond behind our back yard in Bluffton, South Carolina, just over the bridge of Hilton Head Island. Talk about being blessed with a great family, I got lucky!

I have a great business doing what I love to do most. I own a health and fitness studio named CannonFit (appropriate don't you think?) and coach people to achieve success. I have also been a coach of many sports for many years, and consider myself lucky to have had the privilege to work with so many young children, boys and girls, young adults, and grown men and women. I've coached basketball, track and cross country for many different recreation teams, middle schools, high schools and colleges. Doing this makes me the happiest person on earth. Not sure what it is about coaching. I just love connecting with these young athletes and tapping into their potential.

Over the years I have had great mentors and coaches to help me get to where I am today. I owe so much to so many people. I will mention many of them throughout this book and how they have affected me to help me grow in life, in business, in coaching, and so much more. Let's get started.

Over the course of this book I will teach you strategies, and tricks of the trade to help you achieve your dreams in health and fitness. I don't expect anyone to start doing all these strategies, but if you can implement just a few, or maybe add one per month, then you will be better than you were yesterday. And that's what really matters, being just 1% better that you were before (there's a whole section on that in the book).

Now before you really dive into this book and figure out how to transform your body, mind and soul, you need to first start at the beginning. That's figuring out where you are going? You just heard a little bit about where I am in my life. Now it's your turn. "Where you want to be" is in the beginning of the book for a reason, because it's the most important part of the plan. **If you don't know where you're going, then there is no purpose to any of this. You should know where you are going in life, or at least where you truly want to go.** Let me break this down into three main steps. This way you're on the right path to figuring out exactly where you are going?

CHAPTER 2

STEP 1—WHERE DO YOU SEE YOURSELF IF THERE WERE NO LIMITATIONS?

HAVE YOU LOST TWENTY FIVE POUNDS? ARE YOU OFF ALL YOUR major medications? Are you back in high school shape now running in half marathons and being competitive? Are you able to work all day and come home to go right into playing with your kids in the backyard for an hour? Maybe you're down to 15% body fat, wearing a size two, and feeling amazing to start dating again. Maybe you are competing in your very first fitness competition or have reached the pinnacle of the sport you love. Maybe you've completely changed your entire life and are down over one hundred pounds. Maybe you have started a business that you have always dreamed about and are living out your true purpose of helping others. Maybe you have stopped drinking and have turned your life completely around, gained new friends, and found a job that you love. Maybe you have learned how to pay off debt and have found a new game plan to live a better financially, less stressful life. The list goes on and on.

It's hard to figure out where you truly want to go sometimes so let me help break it down a bit. Let's start with your dream. We all have dreams of how we want to be physically and how we want to look, feel and perform on a daily basis. We also see ourselves in the future not just physically, but mentally, and spiritually as well. We all do! You have to tap into those feelings. If there were no limitations, if there was nothing that could stop you, how do you see yourself? That is your dream. This is not something you sit down and think about. Your dream is already there. It takes about two seconds to know what your dream is because it's something that you've wanted for a very long time.

I have a client that I've worked with for a little over four years now named Mackenzee Vance. You will probably know her name in the next five to ten years. You see Mackenzee came to me as a freshman in high school with two goals. 1. To play soccer for UCLA, one of the best college women's soccer programs in the nation. 2. To play soccer professionally. These are the goals she told me in our very first consultation together. I'll never forget it. When I asked her what her main long-term goals were, she looked me dead in the eyes and said "UCLA and go pro"!

As I write this, Mackenzee is in her freshman year playing soccer for the UCLA Bruins. She's always known what she wanted. She has never gone away from those goals. She has been very focused to reach those goals and she has achieved the first part of it. There is no doubt in my mind she will see that last goal come to fruition. I personally see her playing for the U.S. national team someday as I've continuously dropped that vision in her head over the years.

My point is that she had a dream that has always been there. She focused on that dream and with A LOT of hard work day in and day out, she has done what it takes to get there. It was a clear and focused dream. Mackenzee also had a time limit on getting to UCLA, which made things even more focused. Her dreams were set high and she knew it would take everything she had to get there. She didn't have a crazy, drawn out dream. It was short and to the point. That's what your dream should look like, short and to the point. There is no difference between the goal she has and a goal to lose thirty pounds. They are both the dreams of people.

If you are a business owner who just opened a new business, I want to know why you opened it, and what kind of income you see this business ultimately having. You had a reason to open a business and you should have seen yourself in the future earning a certain amount of money from this business. So, as a business owner your dream might be to make $800k in five years. That's a good dream. Short and concise. Get my point? It's not always about health and fitness. A dream is a dream. You might have many dreams in different areas, and having success in one might help another. If you lose weight and start feeling good, you tend to work harder and smarter. It might also go the other way. Sometimes when your job starts going well, you might tend to eat better or workout more. So, all your dreams go hand in hand.

I encourage you to find what your dream is, short and to the point, before you move deeper into this book. Take a few minutes, think about it. Once you know what it is, which shouldn't take long because it's already in that brain of yours, then write it down. Seriously! Don't skip this! **I want you to write down your dream. If there were no limitations, what do you want to achieve?**

CHAPTER 3

STEP 2—YOU MUST BELIEVE IN YOUR DREAM!

A DREAM IS NOT A DREAM UNLESS YOU ACTUALLY BELIEVE IN IT. You've heard it before... If you can dream it then you can achieve it. If you close your eyes and see your dreams in your head actually happening and see yourself having reached where you want to be then YES, it is very possible. If you can't see it, there is nothing really to work towards. You're just working.

I know so many people that go to work on a daily basis with no dream in sight. All they really want is to finish their workday so they can go home. Once they get home their habits are usually unhealthy, like sitting on the couch for a few hours, staying up late and eating a bunch of sugary foods that make them feel like crap, just to do the same thing again the next day. This is not much of a life to me.

I also see many people go into a gym just to get in and get out. I have clients that do their reps way too fast because their goal is to get it done fast so it will be over. Their whole goal was to just get something in and go home to their bad habits. I hate that. I ask people a lot what their goal is today for that particular workout. They look at me like I'm crazy. I ask them "What is your purpose for this workout?" Not what is the purpose to workout, but what's their purpose for this particular workout. What are they trying to achieve today, and why? That's what I want them to think about.

Find your dream, or your purpose. Go get it and live it! I know it's easier said than done, but you have to at least try. This makes me think of all those talent shows on TV where people go on to see if they can live out a lifelong dream. You know those shows where they are interviewed backstage and say how they are tired of working a nine to five job and have always loved performing to people so they decided to give it a shot. The people who go on those shows are the ones that closed their eyes and saw themselves in the future winning the show. Of course, you also have a few crazies that try out just to get noticed!!!

You have to believe that your dream will happen, no matter what. It will just happen. With a lot of hard work, dedication and consistency, it WILL happen. If you don't really believe it, it's not a real dream of yours.

One of my mentors, Gary Smith, a legendary high school cross country and track coach at Thomas Worthington High School in Ohio, whom I was honored to have coached with in the late 1990's, showed me how to teach his athletes to hone in on a season ending goal, a big goal. Something they didn't think could happen at the beginning of the season. He urged them to focus on their goals, even if they didn't think it was possible. About halfway through the season his runners always started to believe it. It was truly an amazing site to see. He just had a way to help people see and go for what they truly wanted. It's time for you to do the same.

CHAPTER 4

STEP 3—KNOW THAT THERE WILL ALWAYS BE OBSTACLES.

WHEN I WAS IN HIGH SCHOOL, I KNEW I WAS GOING TO RUN track in college. I was going to be one of the best long jumpers and long sprinters out there. I just knew it. The problem was I had terrible grades in high school. When I say terrible, I mean TERRIBLE. I graduated with a 1.7 GPA. Not kidding! I had the ability to be a college athlete, but not the brains. At least not back then. I knew that most schools that I really wanted to compete for I could not get into. But thank the lord a few actually accepted me. One school, The University of Rio Grande, a small NAIA school in Rio Grande, Ohio said they would accept me if I passed what they then called the R.E.A.P. Program. I can't tell you what those letters stand for as I really never cared. All I knew was that it was a program for the people that did terrible in high school that still wanted to go to college. That program started three weeks after I graduated from high school and lasted all summer.

On a visit to Rio Grande I met with Coach Bob Willey, the track coach, who I really liked and clicked with and who later become one of my mentors and dear friends. He made me feel like a part of the track family. He also told me I'd have to pass the R.E.A.P. program to make it into the school and once I did, maintain a 2.5 GPA during my entire college career to be able to run for him. Strait forward and to the point; I liked that.

I also met with another school, Ashland University in Ashland, Ohio. It was a bigger and better track program and I really liked the school. I met with Coach Gallagher while on an official visit to the school and liked him a lot. He was honest and straight forward with me. Coach Gallagher said that I had been accepted into the school but I would have to work very hard to stay on his team, meaning with my grades, as well as being able to be as good as the rest of the team. Basically he was saying that his team was very good and it's hard to run for him. I honestly loved coach Gallagher, and thought highly of him and the program he ran, but it always felt like an ultimatum to me. So, I ended up moving into a college dorm three weeks after high school at the University of Rio Grande running for Coach Willey. There were a few other schools in the running, but I either wasn't accepted or it just didn't feel right.

I knew my dream and I knew the obstacle... to stay eligible throughout college. I was the only person out of twenty or so to pass the R.E.A.P. program, which I never once thought I wouldn't pass. I not only sustained a 2.5 GPA throughout my college career to be able to compete as a college track athlete, but also graduated with over a 3.0. There was a dream, and there was an obstacle. I knew there would be one and I ran right through it.

There will always be obstacles in your path with any goal or dream. ALWAYS! If you're on your way to losing weight, and you tear a muscle, do you just give up and quit, or figure out a way to work all the other muscles and keep burning calories? It's going to be your choice and yours alone. You either go after your dream and do whatever it takes, or you retreat and give up. That's on you for the rest of your life.

I never, ever had any doubt that I would compete and graduate from a college. I always knew I would. My parents and other family members weren't so sure, though, as I found out after graduating from Rio Grande. But their opinion never really mattered anyway. It was all about what I thought.

There's a great book I read about a guy named Brian Boyle, called *Iron Heart*. Brian basically came back from the dead after being in a horrific car accident and having his body torn up, to eventually running Ironman triathlons. His story shows real obstacles and how he overcame them. If you've never read this book, read it as it is truly and inspirational story. Better yet, listen to it on Audible. It's much better hearing it personally from him as he describes the whole story. I couldn't stop listening.

And then there's also a book called *Unthinkable*. This is the story of Scott Rigsby, another person that was in a terrible car crash. Scott lost both his legs and went on to achieve greatness by becoming an Ironman just like Brian Boyle. I have had the great pleasure of seeing Scott speak in the church I attend. I spoke with him after the service that day and my family and I were lucky enough to get a picture with him.

These two men had more obstacles in their way than most people can possibly imagine. The things they had to go through and endure to get to where they are today is truly a miracle. The obstacles that I have to go through don't even compare to what these two men had to do.

There are so many examples of obstacles; getting sick for one or two weeks and losing precious workout time. Eating horribly while being sick. It's going to happen. Every year I assume I will be sick two full weeks, either with something small like a bad cold or something big like the flu. I always overestimate that, but I expect it and I have a plan ahead of time if and when it does happen.

Going on vacation is another obstacle. Eating out every day while on vacation isn't a bad thing if you plan ahead for it. Yes, indulge a little, but only a little. Look, it's your dream. If it's a dream you really want you'll find a way around those indulges, but you have to plan for them.

A big obstacle is an injury. In March, April and May of 2020 while my brick and mortar business was closed down because of the COVID-19 pandemic, I decided I was taking my fitness level to new heights from my own home. I set a schedule on Mondays, Wednesdays and Fridays doing strength training, and HIIT style in my backyard or the garage on rainy days. Each day I starting at 9 AM on the nose. On Tuesdays, Thursdays and Saturdays I was on the road for interval run/walks, again starting at 9 AM. Sundays were my active recovery days, meaning I went for a long two-three mile power-walk. This time was earlier, usually around 6:30 or 7 AM because I wanted to see the sunrise on my walk. This was a meditation type of walk for me. It got my mind in the right place. I also played A LOT of basketball with my two sons during those months usually in the evenings.

On the Sunday of May 17th my son Calem and I were out late playing some hard core one-on-one B-Ball when I felt my knee wasn't moving the way I wanted it to move. It kind of felt like an elephant stepped on my knee. I had to stop. The next morning I woke up and immediately knew something was wrong. I could barely move my knee. Laterally I couldn't move at all. I waited three weeks to see if it healed with a lot of ice and rehab, but to no avail. Eventually I saw a doctor, had an MRI and found that I tore my meniscus on both the lateral side and medial side of the knee. I tried physical therapy, but ended up needing surgery to repair the tears three and a half months after the initial injury happened. One week after the surgery I was feeling great, like a new man who was ready to tackle life again. One week after that however, things just weren't feeling right and I started going downhill with my physical therapy sessions. I didn't know what was going on, nor did my physical therapists. I just kept getting worse. During my six-week follow up session with the surgeon, he just blamed it on osteoarthritis and brushed it off. Not me! I knew something wasn't quite right so I saw a new doctor, had more MRI's and turns out I had huge chunks of scar tissue form after the last surgery. Some of the chunks were lodged under my kneecap which limited any knee range of motion while standing. Six months after my first knee surgery I was under the knife again getting those pieces of scar tissue out.

By the way, during this time I never once stopped working out. I never missed my 9am workouts. I did however adjust those workouts accordingly doing mainly upper body exercises. I'm about to make this a really long story so get ready as it gets very interesting...

During this time I had read the book "Can't Hurt Me" by David Goggins, a former Navy Seal that has gone through Seal training many times, run more marathons and ultramarathons than you and I can fathom, and set a world record for pull-ups in a 24 hour period. Great book by the way! Very inspirational to say the least, but quite a lot of curse words so get used to those if you plan on reading it.

After reading his book and being inspired, I was feeling like I needed to compete at something again. From being very disabled in my legs for so long I decided to see if my body was even capable to go for some type of world record like pull-ups or push-ups. After all, my upper body was in tip top shape at this point. So, I started to see what I could do. I did start slowly doing just ten push-ups, walking around my studio for about fifteen seconds, then did five pull-ups. I did this non-stop until I got to one hundred push-ups and fifty pull-ups. Honestly that was easy for me. I did this every other day (three times per week) for one week. I then moved it up to fifteen push-ups and ten pull-ups the next week, and so on. Each week moving each exercise up by five reps. I believe I got up to around eight hundred push-ups and six hundred pull-ups each workout, or somewhere around there. Honestly, I was doing great and starting to tell myself maybe I am ready to challenge myself for some type of record. Then... of course the obstacle came. I started getting this little twinge in my left shoulder. It wasn't anything big, so I kept working through it. It ended up getting worse and worse before I had to stop all upper body exercises all together, just in case it turned into something really bad. However, when I stopped, a bigger obstacle arose! My shoulder froze up big time! If you've ever had a frozen shoulder you would know how painful it is and how it is to be unable to move your arm at all.

Okay, the end of the long story... When I went in to have my second knee surgery with the second doctor, I also had my shoulder fixed. And back to physical therapy I went for both my knee and my shoulder. I even found a new physical therapist who was great! Scott Kathmann, from Elite Physical Therapy, you were great! Thank you for being a great therapist!

So, talk about obstacles! I had some big ones. At this point I could barely do any leg exercises, except for rehabilitation type stuff and all upper body exercising was out also. As a fitness guy I was now a non fitness guy for about three months. I did the best I could, and stuck to my workout schedule doing only what I could, mainly stretching and rehab type exercises. But I did keep going! That was something I just needed to do for my mindset.

My point is that we all go through so many obstacles. All of us. How we deal with those obstacles is what sets us apart. Some just decide to shut everything down completely. Others find a way to keep going and fight. What will you do when an obstacle arises, which they will, over and over? Plan ahead and expect those obstacles to pop up. Honestly, just start to expect them. Sometimes it may seem like the world just doesn't want you to attain your goals because of everything that gets in the way. But that's just life. Plan ahead with what you can do when obstacles hit. Be ready for them and fight through them!

CHAPTER 5

WHAT IS YOUR "WHY POWER"?

ABOUT FIVE YEARS AGO I WAS HAVING LUNCH WITH MY GOOD friend Pastor Jonathan Riddle. Jonathan is a Pastor at Church of the Cross in Bluffton, South Carolina, where I have been attending church for many years. He had asked me to lunch because I had just started coaching again after a thirteen year hiatus after opening my brick and mortar business. I had finally made some time to get back into it as a volunteer. Jonathan knew many of the kids on the track team that I was coaching as he has been mentoring them for a while.

During this lunch meeting Jonathan asked me a great question. He said "Why do you want to get back into coaching?" It was a pretty straight forward question but I knew he needed a deep answer. I'm going to give you that answer in a bit so hang tight. I promise I'll come back to it.

Have you ever heard the song "The Climb" by Miley Cyrus? I personally love that song. I love it because the words in the song describe how the climb is more important than the end result and how there will always be obstacles in the way, how we will always want to move those obstacles, and sometimes we are even going to lose in the process of attaining our dreams. But what we will always remember the most is how we got to the end result... The Climb. It's not about the weight you lose or how fast you ran the race. It's really about the process that got you to achieve those things. Your dream is very important, and you should continually have dreams. But remember that it's what you learned about yourself along the way, and how you grew as a person, became a stronger, better person because of what you went through to achieve those dreams is what matters most. Not the actual achievement.

Something I use with my own clients is what I call the five why's. The five why's are basically layers of answers. So, when someone tells me their dream or goal, I then ask them why do they want to achieve that. They answer. Then I ask again why they want to achieve that. They again answer with a little deeper answer. And I ask why again. This process usually takes about five times of me asking why to each of their answers, or five layers until an emotional response comes through.

You really need to dig down deep on this. If you told me your goal was to lose weight, I would then ask "why?". You might say something like "to get healthy and feel good". Again I would ask "why?". You might say "because I'm now on so many medications from being overweight, and I'm always tired and want that to change." I might respond with "why do you want those to change?". You then say something like "because my kids see me as a lazy, overweight parent that's always tired and that's not how I want them to remember me. I want them to see me as someone they would admire, not someone they would be afraid of becoming." So then I would say "So the reason you came to me is because you don't want your kids to think of you as a tired, run down, lazy person who they might be afraid of becoming themselves. Is that right?" You would then break out into tears and say "yes, that's exactly the reason why.". That is a true "Why." You need to find your Why. It's the real reason for your purpose.

So back to my answer from the question Pastor Jonathon Riddle asked; Why did I want to get back into coaching? My answer was simple. Because I missed the day to day grind, the process of seeing these young adults grow from defeats and failures to successes and wins. It wasn't seeing them earn a medal. It was about the climb. I missed that. That was my why power. That still is my "why power" to this day. I dug down deep for those answers, just like I ask my own clients to do.

Let me tell you three reasons, my Why Power for being in the health profession as long as I have been. These reasons are things that are always in my head. And I mean ALWAYS! First, way back in my early days of becoming a personal trainer I remember sitting in my Grandparents' kitchen in Upper Arlington, Ohio having a nice talk with my Grandpa about my future. When I say "nice" I mean I was nicely listening to him tell me that I better make good choices about my future in his threatening kind of tone. I remember him asking me what I was going to do for the rest of my life. Since I was a newly certified personal trainer of course I said, "I'm going to be a personal trainer". Now before I tell you what happened next you need to know that in those days being a personal trainer was not at all a profession. It was a joke job, at least in my world, and was considered to be a part time thing that wouldn't last very long.

What happened next changed my life forever. I distinctively remember my grandpa, who I loved and admired more than anything, say to me "Son, fitness is not a profession! You'll never make anything of yourself in the fitness industry!" I also remember looking back at him straight into his eyes, at least I did in my mind, and said back to him "Yes I will! Just watch me!" In that moment I decided to prove him wrong and prove to everyone that fitness and helping people was what I was going to do forever.

That is not the best "Why" in the world, but I will say that it has driven me to stay in the fitness industry as a true profession. And honestly, because my grandpa knew me so well, I believe that maybe he said all that on purpose because he knew deep inside that what he said would drive me to prove him wrong. He was a very smart man you know.

My second "why" came in 2008 when I became the owner of Shaping Concepts, now known as CannonFit. Just over two years earlier in late 2005, I opened the doors of Shaping Concepts as the manager, director, marketing director and trainer. I was the only employee besides the owner who lived two hours away. It was basically me, myself and I. I built that business from the ground up. I learned how to be a business person from the owner, Shane Doll in the process before taking over as owner two years into it, which was the initial plan.

In 2008 business was booming and everything was great when I bought it from Shane. Then right away the economy crashed. I'm sure Shane was thinking ahead and got out before everything went sour. Probably smart on his part. But I pushed through, made changes and am still in business. Right after I took over as full owner, I had a meeting with some other local business owners to learn and get advice. One person, who I won't name, specifically told me that the goal is to make it to the five year mark. If I make it to the five year mark, then I've made it. Well, from then on that was my purpose. Now that I'm older and wiser I will say that even though that drove me to stay in business, that was a terrible goal. But, that is what it was and however bad of a goal it was it did drive me to stay in business.

My third "why" is the main reason I continue to be the person I am today, which is a true health professional that wants to help people live the best life possible.

Back in the early days, after I took over as owner of Shaping Concepts I received a terrible call in the middle of the night from my mother. My father had a bad stroke. Long story short, I spent the next few months driving from South Carolina to Ohio and back many times as he was in and out of many hospitals. I'm not sure he even knew what was going on. In fact, for a long time he didn't even wake up. During this time the main thing I remember is not what he was going through. It wasn't the feeding tube or the ventilator or the nurses constantly changing his sheets. I'll tell you what I remember the most. It's the thing that drives me today. It's my true why power. It was watching my mother sit by his side hour after hour, day after day, month after month. She hardly ate, except for the occasional fast food. She didn't move her own body because of sitting by his bedside for so long. She became very unhealthy herself. I remember that she was tired all the time, and looked it too. She also looked so unhealthy and just flat out miserable.

After a few months my father died and it honestly took years before my mother started to really live her life again. She lost years of her life. I am so proud of her as she has bounced back from that. Not many people could get through that. She did. It's been just over fourteen years since my father passed and my mother is doing great. It's still hard and I'm sure there is not a day that goes by where she doesn't think about him and those hard times.

My sole purpose in life is to stop those times from happening to other people. I don't want spouses and other family members sitting in a hospital chair, wasting their own lives away next to someone in a bed with their own health problems. I admire people who do that, but I don't want to see it anymore. I know I can't stop it as there will always be people sick, injured and more. But if I can stop this from happening to just one person, I'm living out my purpose.

You must find your "Why Power". It's not easy to find your "Why Power" and it might change over the years. But once you find it, let it drive you! It's got to be an emotional reason. It's got to be meaningful. It's not always easy to figure out and it's definitely not easy to face it, but you have to.

CHAPTER 6

FINDING WHAT YOU FEAR THE MOST.

I'T'S THE THING YOU FEAR THE MOST ABOUT BEING UNHEALTHY AND not fit. Are you afraid to have your kids see you in a way you don't want them to? Or afraid your spouse might think less of you? Or losing something because of your health, like a job, your spouse, your life? What are you most afraid of? Close your eyes and find what that is. It's in there, I promise.

If you can find your fear of what's holding you back, you can then admit to yourself that that is truly your fear and attack it with a plan. Attacking your fear has such an important impact on how your transformation will go. Make this a priority.

I have many fears, some for myself, but most for my children. For myself, I've feared losing my business, not being able to feed the family, not being able to do the things I love to do. I fear heights... a lot! I also fear that things will happen to my kids. I think that last one just comes naturally when you become a parent.

These aren't the type of fears I'm talking about. I'm talking more about a fear that is holding you back from the goals you really want. Most people fear failure. That's pretty natural, but I've learned that the more you fail, the more you learn, and eventually you'll have success.

The great motivational speaker, and my favorite speaker of all time, Les Brown said "When life knocks you down, try to land on your back. Because if you can look up, you can get up. Let that reason get you back up.". If you can get up that puts you closer to a victory.

Not that I want to fail, but I've actually learned to look for my failures just to try to figure out what I can learn from them. Crazy I know, but over the last five or ten years I have this vast craving for more and more knowledge. I just want to learn more because I know it will eventually get me to another victory in some part of my life. The more I try things, the more I might fail. But I keep learning from those failures.

Find your deepest fears, the ones that are holding you back from accomplishing your dreams and goals. Once you know what those fears are, you then can tackle them. Before you tackle them, you have to know what they are. Find them!

CHAPTER 7

WHAT'S YOUR PURPOSE IN DOING THIS?

IT'S BASICALLY THE ANSWER TO YOUR "WHY"... WANTING YOUR KIDS to see you as a hard worker, someone who they admire and want to emulate. Wanting your spouse to see you as heroic and as a hard-working family man or woman. That's the kind of reason I'm talking about.

Here is a great lesson I learned about myself a few years back. My wife and I were on a three day retreat together up in the beautiful North Carolina mountains with about twenty other people that were in a business my wife and I were involved in at the time. The leaders and mentors of this retreat were good friends of ours, Rod and Lynnea Imhoff, and are still great friends today. In fact, I consider them family.

One of the things that Lynnea had all of us do was come up with one positive word about each person at the retreat. Now I was pretty close to about half the people there. The other half I either knew of or had just met that weekend. Lynnea had a large white frame with a small mirror in the middle of the frame for each person there. Each frame had an individual name on it, so we all had our own frame. We each took a marker, walked to each frame and wrote on that person's frame the one positive word that we thought best described them in our opinion. This was a tough, but eye-opening experience.

When I picked up my frame after everyone had signed it I WAS OVERWHELED! I didn't know who wrote what word. All I saw were positive words. Words like inspiring, encourager, supportive, persistent, determined, motivator, positive, resilient, patient, visionary. All words on how people saw me. I have this frame hung up in my studio now right in front of my office, so every time I walk in my office I see it. It's a great reminder of how everything you do or say reflects you in different ways.

At the end of that evening, I really wanted to know which word my wife wrote. I was trying to figure it out from the handwriting, but I couldn't. I flat out asked her. The word she wrote about me... heroic. I immediately teared up, of course trying to hold my tears back in front of everyone, but it was hard. She saw me at that time as heroic. That just blew my mind! I certainly did not see myself that way. Since then, my purpose for many things has been to be heroic, to be a hero to as many people as possible. That's hard to live up to. I highly suggest you get some close friends and not so close friends together and do the same thing. This lesson will change your life! It changed mine and I will never, ever forget it! Thank you Lynnea!!!

You need to find your purpose. However, this is something that doesn't happen overnight. It may take years, sometimes almost a lifetime to figure out. Other people might have an easy time knowing what they were put on this great Earth to do. Some people just know what their purpose is. Remember that purposes change though. As we grow as people our purposes tend to change over time, often many times over, which is perfectly fine. I know many people that start college beginning with one track of study, then finish college with a different degree. Our purpose is kind of the same. It may stay the same or it may change, which is usually a good thing. To me it means we grew and learned more about ourselves.

CHAPTER 8

WHAT WILL YOUR LEGACY BE?

Personally, I don't see legacy as an end all. People say live your life so others will remember you in a certain way. That will be your legacy. I see legacy as something you pass on to others. If I can pass on things like work ethic, attitude, being an inspiration to others, making an impact on others, always having a positive mindset, being an ambassador of what you believe in, being a Christian, those to me are what I want my legacy to be.

Another mentor of mine, who I will bring up again in this book is Todd Durkin, another trainer/coach out in San Diego, CA, suggests looking at what people would write on your tombstone if you died tomorrow. How will you be remembered by the people you come in contact with? Would it be something inspiring or something no one really cares about, or even something not so good? The good news is that if you are still reading this book, you are still writing and working on your legacy. Be the person who you want others to see you as. It's not about being the richest, or most famous. It is about how many people you have made an impact on. How many people have you inspired to make positive changes in their lives? **What is your legacy going to be? I suggest before you move on to the next** chapter to take a few minutes and write down what you want your **tombstone saying to be.** It could be a one liner, a few short phrases, a paragraph, or maybe just one word.

This is what I want mine to say:

Chad Cannon
1971-2081
Father—Husband—Coach—Mentor
Inspired millions towards success

Notice the years. Yes, that would make me 110 years old. Why? Because I only give 110% to everything.

CHAPTER 9

THE PLAN—REVERSE ENGINEERING

NOW THAT YOU KNOW WHERE YOU'RE GOING, OR AT LEAST MIGHT have an idea of what your dream is and why you truly want that particular thing, it's time to make a plan. It's time to write out the plan on how to make all this happen. It's certainly not an easy task, but I'm going to break this down for you so it seems much easier. I highly suggest you get a pen and paper and write all this down as I go through it. A plan is not saying I'm going to start exercising more and eating less. A plan is a very specific thing. This week I'm going to do... Next week I'm going to do... But very detailed. You must plan for achieving your *ultimate goal* backwards.

I was taught long ago, by whom, I really have no idea, to reverse engineer your goals. This means looking at your ultimate goal or dream and working backwards to figure out what it will take to make it happen. I've been doing this most of my life.

For example: If my ultimate goal were to lose one hundred pounds in twelve months, I would work backwards and figure out how much weight I needed to lose per month. You have to have a time limit or this won't work. Take one hundred divided by twelve months. This equals just over eight pounds per month. Now the mind doesn't work like that. The mind will say "One hundred pounds! That's a lot and that's super hard to do". It's totally negative. But when you see eight pounds a month, mentally that seems a lot easier. Let's make this sound even better...

How about breaking it down weekly? Take one hundred divided by fifty two weeks. That's just under two pounds per week. Is that doable now? Now it's not such a negative thought. It now turned into a positive, and I'm now thinking "I can do that". You've completely changed your thinking from something seeming impossible to very possible. Mindset is everything. If you see one hundred pounds in front of you, it seems like a large and almost impossible task. But if you see just under two pounds per week, that's a whole different story.

I'm about to blow your mind! What if we broke it down daily? Take one hundred pounds divided by three hundred sixty five days. That equals a weight loss of 0.27 pounds per day. Anyone can do that! Talk about a positive mindset. Now achieving your dream seems easy!

I have heard that most millionaires earned their money in whatever field, industry, or even sport they are in, by doing this with their own businesses, industries, or sport. They reverse engineer. It's not all about health and fitness. Reverse engineering can be used in just about every aspect of life.

When I was a track athlete, back in the olden days, I used to set season ending goals, meaning what I really wanted to accomplish that season or that year. Based on the ultimate goal, I used reverse engineering to come up with my training schedule for the entire season. I knew my goal and I worked backwards, month by month, week by week, day by day to come up with a plan of action. I knew when my body should peak and when my body should be tired each day, week, and month. If I planned it right, I would achieve my goal, or at least be darn close.

Use the method of reverse engineering with your own goal to come up with your own plan of action. This will help tremendously. Start with your end accomplishment and work backwards to make your own plan, monthly, weekly, and daily.

CHAPTER 10

TIME MANAGEMENT IS EVERYTHING. WORKING IN BLOCKS

WHEN YOU ARE TRYING TO REACH A GOAL, TIME ALWAYS SEEMS to go fast. It just seems as if there is never enough time to get everything you want to get accomplished into your already busy day. I learned from my mentor Todd Durkin, who I mentioned before, maybe from one of his podcasts or YouTube videos years and years ago, how to "Block" your time. This strategy has changed my life forever. Blocking time is simple and gives us more time to get everything done, and ample time to recover. Here's how it works...

First, you have to figure out what your magic times are. I call them the magic times because those are the time where you make magic happen, or times when you get stuff done! You need to know what times in the day your brain works really well. This is when you comprehend things the most, or when you are most creative. You need to know what time of day that you are physically at your best. You need to know when your body and mind needs a time out. You need to know what time of day is spent with family, and what time of day is crucial to your job. Once you know these things, you can block out certain times throughout every day to work on different things.

For some odd reason my mind has, for the last thirty years, been at its optimum energy level in the early morning between 5:30AM and 10AM. My mind is great until about 9AM, then I need what I call a mindful time out. During this optimum energy level time, before my mindful time out I go through my morning ritual. I get up around 5:00AM. My alarm is set for 5:15AM, but I rarely make it that long and end up getting up before the alarm goes off. I get dressed right away, eat a healthy breakfast, which I will talk about later in the book, all in the span of about fifteen minutes. Eating my breakfast is my morning fuel! I feel it right away as the food going in is feeding my energy levels big time! Then I'm out the door to work. I get up and go! I never waste time reading the paper or scrolling through social media. I will sometimes check out ESPN for a score or two from the night before, but that's just for five minutes while I'm eating. I just don't get distracted by anything. Once on the road on the way to work, I'll listen to one of three things; either a book on Audible, a podcast, or an inspirational speech from someone famous on YouTube. Every day is different, but it's always educational and motivating. You see I don't ever put anything negative in my mind in the morning because I have to be inspiring at 5:50AM when I start seeing clients roll in the doors in my studio. If I'm inspired, I can inspire my clients. If I filled my mind with stuff in the paper or on the news such as a shooting that happened last night or a tragedy that happened across the country, or something political between the parties, things I have no control over, how is that going to help me be super motivating to my clients that come to me for positive, inspiring coaching?

I have to get my mind right for me, and for my clients before I ever see anyone. Many times I'll start the book, podcast or YouTube video while eating breakfast before I ever get on the road. This gives me fifteen to thirty minutes of being amped up by something inspirational, energetic, impactful, or educational before my day even begins, before I ever see a soul each day. I have been doing this morning routine for years and I cannot tell you how much more positive my mindset is than it was before I started doing this. It's ten thousand times better!

My work time, meaning training and coaching clients, is from 6:00AM to 1:00PM. This is when I'm at my best when it comes to creativity and having the most energy in my day. I'm much more motivating in the beginning in the day than I am late in the day.

I do, however, always take a break at 9:00AM to re-energize. This is my "ME" time. This is when I get in my workout between clients. I only have forty five minutes between clients so it's "get to it" time! It's get focused time. Building muscle and increasing my heart rate gets me going after a couple hours of coaching others up. Then at 9:45AM it's back to coaching others for a few more hours.

Usually around 1:00PM my training/coaching time for me is over in my studio. I'll take care of some studio things like some fast cleaning, doing the trash, that sort of thing. Then it's time to fuel up for lunch back at the homestead. By this time I'm pretty tired because I'm so energized and hyped up at work in the mornings, so by the time 1:00 rolls around, mentally I'm exhausted and need some down time. This means it's time to fuel up with a healthy lunch, catch up on my social media posts, which are very intentional for marketing purposes. I might scroll social media a little while eating, but try not to get sucked in for too long. I usually set a time limit for fifteen minutes just to chill out. After a good meal to get my energy back up and get my mind going again, it's back to my office, which is conveniently at home, mainly working on marketing. I'll talk more about my office later.

I have my days blocked off into getting certain things done. On Mondays, Wednesdays, and Fridays I'm writing for about thirty minutes, either on this book, blogs, or coaching emails, etc. On Tuesdays and Thursdays, I'm paying bills, updating the website, making phone calls, and planning ahead. So the time between 1:30-2:30 is much more calming, and a re-energizing time for me. After a long morning of being focused and high energy I need this calming time.

About 2:00PM it's time for what I call recovery. This is when I put on my headphones and listen to a book on Audible while getting on my home spin bike or elliptical for about thirty minutes. I follow this with a very relaxing stretch time for another thirty minutes, still listening to a good educational, or inspirational book that I will learn something from. Sometimes, my stretching lasts a bit longer or I'm following it with some massage with my PureWave massage gun or the PowerDot Tens unit. I will discuss those later on as well.

During the summer months, when my kids are home from school, as well as my wife because she's a teacher, I admit that it's a lot harder for me. I don't stick to my schedule very well at all when I get home. That's something I still need to work on.

Around 3:30 it's time to get to the thing that really gets my mind right, gets me energized, and gets me motivated. It's the thing that I really love to do! I get to go work with and coach high school kids. I coach both boys and girls cross country, track and girls basketball at May River High School in Bluffton, South Carolina. I love doing this! It's a passion of mine. When I opened my brick and mortar business back in 2005, I stopped coaching. After about five years, I really started to miss it, but never had the chance to get back to it. Finally in 2018 I decided it was time. In fact I still didn't really have time, I just made the time. I decided to volunteer as a track coach at May River a few times per week and during the Saturday meets. At the end of that season, the head coach, Katherine Rosenblum, asked me to come on full time as an assistant cross country and track coach. It was a big jump time wise, but again, I made the time because I loved working with young motivated student athletes. I owe a lot to Katherine for letting me come on board. Getting back into coaching was one of the best moves of my entire life.

One day during the next cross country season there was a thunderstorm outside so we were forced to run the hallways of the school, which is where I ran into the girls head basketball coach, Jermaine Bigham. We started talking and I told him that I used to coach basketball. One thing led to another and I was then a part of the girls varsity basketball program as well as cross country and track & field. I was suddenly coaching high school sports all school year long, and I love every bit of it.

Now this year has been a bit different, as I had to have a knee surgery in the middle of cross country season from my meniscus tear. Because of this, I decided not to coach basketball this year. I wanted to focus my time of watching my wife coach her middle school basketball team at Cross Schools, and watch my older son play on his middle school and JV basketball teams, also for Cross Schools. Between the two of them, I'm watching a lot of basketball. I still miss coaching the May River girls, though, and plan on getting back into it.

After the coaching time is done each day, it's time to head home, for family time, dinner, homework with the kids, catching up, and getting ready for the next day. Sometimes I'll get in some more recovery time, stretching and more massage as well. I have been making everyone (wife and all three kids) their lunches ever since Tracey and I got married, so after getting lunches made for the next day and getting Emerson to bed, I'm done. By 9:00PM my brain and body are ready to shut down. I get my shower in, crawl into bed, sometimes by 9:30, and read or listen to Audible again for another thirty minutes. Sometimes I'll catch up on some ESPN also. Usually by 10:00PM, it's lights out!

Now each day is a little different. It's always intended to be structured in this way, but it definitely varies. Kids' activities, mom and dad activities, and many different things get in the way of regular planned routines, but I have blocked out time for each thing. I know the time of day when I think best, when I'm more amped up and motivational, when I need quiet time, when I need to "recover and rejuvenate" and time to just focus on office work. I know when the best family time is. I have narrowed down each part to certain times of the day that work best for me or for the family. I then simply block time for those particular things. Most of the time I can stick to it, but there are many times where it's still very chaotic. But at least I have it planned out to be structured and that really helps me. For me, if I don't have things planned out nothing gets done.

Figure out your body schedule; when you have more energy, when you do your best thinking and are most creative, when your family time is, when you're at your best for focus, and when your body needs recovery. Put them into blocks throughout the day. Write them down in your calendar, or your daily planner. This is your planned time management. By doing this you will get more done than ever before. You'll workout when its best for you, during your most energized time. When you need time to relax, you can get more reading done, or recover with stretching or massage. When your creative mind is at it's best you can get more paperwork done. These may be just thirty minutes long or possibly two hours long. It all depends on you and how your body works.

This is a game changer. When I started this practice I started getting things done. If you've ever seen a basketball practice at most levels, or any sport for this matter, the coach has a written out schedule for every practice. The first twenty minutes is form shooting. The next ten minutes is conditioning. The next twenty minutes is defensive drills. Then another ten minutes of conditioning. Ten minutes of free throws. Thirty minutes of strategizing for the next team, fifteen minutes for offense, and fifteen minutes for defense. It's a planned out practice, instead of just winging it as you go. Get the point? This needs to be done in your daily plan as well. Start doing this and your life will change forever.

CHAPTER 11

BREAKING THROUGH YOUR OBSTACLES

BREAKING THROUGH OBSTACLES IS SOMETHING YOU'RE GOING TO have to do, over and over again. Earlier I told you about how there will be obstacles that come up. And trust me, they will. There will always be obstacles and you have to expect them before ever starting on your goal. It's how you take on those obstacles that matters. It's how you face adversity that will either make or break you. There has to be one mindset when an obstacle arises. That mindset is that you will break through that obstacle sooner or later. It WILL happen! It might take a long time, or it might be no time at all, but you WILL break through, no matter what! Injuries go away. Being sick goes away. Vacations end. Plateaus end. One bad meal is just one meal away from the next good meal. You will break through that infamous obstacle wall. You must have the mindset of a champion, not a weak mindset that crumbles when every little bad thing happens. Even the biggest, best brick wall eventually comes crashing down. Remember to expect obstacles and have a mindset of a champion that will sooner or later break down all obstacles.

One of my favorite all time football players is Drew Brees. I have been lucky enough to hear him speak in person. His book; Coming

Back Stronger tells his whole story. If you know anything about Drew you might know that he had a terrible shoulder injury very early in his professional career, right when he was still fighting to keep the starting position with the San Diego Chargers. This injury could have ruined his career, and his mindset, but he believed in himself as did one team that took a chance on him, the New Orleans Saints. This shoulder injury could have stopped him, as most people would have hung their shoes up forever, but not Drew Brees. As we all know Drew has a champion's mindset and has overcome so much, to have a Hall Of Fame career and lead his team to a Super Bowl championship. He overcame a major obstacle by pushing through. There is no difference between him and you. His obstacle took a very long time to overcome and look how far he has come. You can do the same.

Being patient is a crucial part when breaking through any obstacle. This is the part where most people lay down and give up. You are NOT one of those people. You are someone that WILL overcome whatever you are going through. You ARE the person that will power through that brick wall sooner or later. Keep hammering at that brick wall, over and over again. The more times you hit that wall, it cracks inside, little by little. Eventually it WILL fall down.

Being patient is hard and every obstacle takes patience. Patience always takes time, usually more time than you want. This is the time where you will grow as a person. This is the time where you will focus more on the little things that later you might find out are the bigger ones, like focusing on mental toughness with educational reading, watching motivational videos and movies, inspiring others, journaling and more. Don't forget about focusing on stretching and better eating habits.

Obstacles might seem like bad things, but maybe they are actually glimmers of hope that make you a better person. I've always thought of obstacles as things I have to get out of the way as fast as I can, until recently. Now I see obstacles as things that will make me better and grow as a person.

Expect that things will happen and plan for them. It's a part of life. Things always pop up when least expected. Be okay with that and push through it. You will get sick. You will go out of town. You will have visitors come see you. You will have injuries to work through. Plan ahead and work through all these.

CHAPTER 12

MINDSET IS EVERYTHING

A LITTLE STORY ABOUT *MINDSET*...
My middle school track coach, Jeff McGarvey, made such a big impression on me at such an early age. Coach McGarvey, a teacher and track coach at Dublin Middle School, in Dublin, Ohio took over as head track coach during my 8th grade year. If it weren't for him being a huge part of my life for those three months, I doubt I would have gone anywhere in life. He taught me what mindset was really about. Coach McGarvey was the ultimate optimist. He knew he could do anything if he put his mind to it, and it showed. He always had the biggest smile on his face and was a little bit crazy. I remember one day at practice he was watching the pole vaulters, an event he knew nothing about. The vaulters were egging him on to try it. They told him exactly what to do, how to do it, and he really wanted to try it. If you've ever watched the pole vault you might know it's quite dangerous and scary. Well not for my Super Coach, Coach McGarvey. That man grabbed a pole, went about forty feet back on the runway, visualized exactly what the vaulters told him to do, took off running, stuck the pole in the box and all I remember is how he flew over that bar with the biggest grin on his face. He cleared whatever height it

was, by a lot. It was truly an amazing feet just to watch. This man had never vaulted before. I don't think he had ever even held a pole vault pole before that day.

A few minutes later he came over to help me on my long jump technique and I remember asking how he made it over that bar. To this day I remember that he said back to me something like... I just saw myself going over that bar, clearing it by a mile in my head before I took off. Then I remember him saying "I knew I was going to make it."

From that day forward I started seeing my future before I did something. I started the technique of *visualization*. I have visualized myself accomplishing things before I did them. I started doing it with my long jumping. I stood on the long jump runway before my jumps, and in my head went through every step, the takeoff, the flight, and the landing. I saw it happen before I actually did it. I then started doing that with my running events. It took me a lot longer to figure out that it also works in everything you do in life. Visualization is almost a trance like meditation. It's putting yourself in the future and seeing things happen the way you want them to. It doesn't always work out, trust me. But if you can see it, you can do it! That's one of my mantras I've said for years. You should use it too. If you can see it, you can do it!

Visualization is easier to do with sports; however I've walked people through years of life changing body transformations with visualization before they ever started on their goals. I've done this for a long time, and it works! If you can see yourself down forty pounds in tight fitting clothing that looks great on you, playing with your kids in the backyard, running 5K road races, eating clean, healthy foods and inspiring others to do the same, guess what? It's possible, because you saw it. That's visualization. That's a big part of you getting results. If you can visualize yourself in the future with all your goals and dreams accomplished, then it truly is possible. There has to be no doubt in your mind. None! You either see it or you don't. It's not about thinking it's possible that you might be able to accomplish your dream. It's about seeing it, believing it, and doing whatever it takes to get it. No matter what. It's about going after it, until it happens. No matter what!

Visualization takes time. It's definitely a learned process, but very doable. I believe this is a top priority when it comes to living a healthy, fit life. This is your mindset and your mindset is everything. If your mind isn't in "glass half full" mode, achieving your goals is going to be very hard. Most people go through a weight loss journey with the mindset of "glass half empty." That's why we see so much of America being overweight and obese. Most people want to be healthy and fit, but don't think it's possible for them. Don't let that be you! You are better than that! You are worth it! You need to fight for it!

There was one other time that I got a huge lesson from Coach McGarvey. It was on Friday, May 9th, 1986. I remember it like it was yesterday, because it was also my birthday and we had a big two-day track meet starting that afternoon called the Bexley Relays. It was a meet I had been waiting for all year long because the Bexley Relays had an event called the Pentathlon. This is where each team had one person to compete in five different events, kind of like the decathlon in the Olympics. I remember that I told Coach that I was doing the Pentathlon this year. I didn't really give him a choice. He never fought me on it either, so I guess he was okay with it. The year before, as a seventh grader, I remember watching my friend and someone I really looked up to, Jeff McCutchen, compete in this Pentathlon for our school. I don't remember what place he ended up, but I do remember that I wanted to do that Pentathlon the next year. The events were the high jump, long jump (long jump was my specialty), discus, a 200 meter sprint (also something I was good at), and the mile run.

Before the meet started, I was of course at school. It was a good day simply because it was my Birthday and I was really focused on competing that night. I remember I was in band class. Yes, I was in band. I played the tuba, although not so well, if you can imagine me holding that big thing. The door opened in the middle of band class and a big adult size clown walked in. Yes, I said a clown! This clown was holding about fifteen to twenty big balloons and I remember everyone started laughing, including me. Then it hit me! It was my birthday and this clown started walking directly towards me. He stood right next to me and started singing the Happy Birthday song and everyone of course joined in. I was the most embarrassed kid you had ever seen. However, I think because it was in front of the entire band, probably around seventy or eighty people, it just put the biggest smile on my face. I didn't know what to do with all the balloons that the clown gave me, so I asked the band director if I could go put them in my track coaches room since I would see him after school. He let me do this knowing something that I didn't. When I arrived at my coach's classroom he was expecting me. He knew I would bring these balloons to his room for some reason. With his big smile and him laughing at me he told me that he and my parents planned the whole thing because he knew it would put me in a good mood that day before the track meet.

You see, my coach and my parents implanted a good mood within me. They gave me a certain mindset that I needed that day. That little gesture gave me tons of energy and took the pressure off me that they knew I put on myself. It was the best thing ever! And guess what? I performed great. Mindset is contagious.

Whatever you are about to head into; a meeting at work, a school test, a sports competition, a workout, planning dinner, playing with your kids, you must have the best mindset possible. A negative mindset brings negative results. And it totally and completely affects others. One negative person on a team can crush a team, even if that person never plays. The same goes anywhere else. If your negative mindset is around while playing with your kids, guess what happens?

Your kids then have a negative mindset. Then you probably end up yelling at them. Trust me, I've done it. If you don't think you need to be at the team meeting, but your boss makes you and you enter the room with a negative attitude, then that attitude spreads like a cold to other people in the room.

Mindset is everything! **Start training your mind with visualization. Close your eyes for five full minutes and see yourself accomplishing everything you really want to accomplish. See yourself attaining and crushing those goals you have. See it in your head first. Then once you can see it, start going after it.**

CHAPTER 13

TRAIN TO WIN MINDSET

"YOU PLAY TO WIN THE GAME." DO YOU REMEMBER THE NFL coach who said that? It was Herm Edwards, the then New York Jets Head Coach. Herm had a very emotional and memorable press conference after a game and said that quote which will always be remembered. He has since been taunted, ridiculed, and joked at because of that quote. But you know what? He was right. He had the mindset of winning; that was the goal. It didn't always work out that way, but that was and still is always his goal. I'm sure that's how he coaches all his teams.

Too many times people just go through the motions, which gets you nowhere fast. Do you go through your workouts just going through the motions, just to get it in? I'm sure you have at some point. We all have. But on a consistent basis, is this how you approach your workouts? Be honest. If so, we are about to change that.

What we need in our brains to accomplish our dreams is a train to win mindset or attitude. There must be a goal or a purpose for each and every workout. If that goal was achieved that day, it's a WIN! It's a VICTORY! It's SUCCESS! The more WINS you have, the closer to your dreams you become. This is with everything you do, not just with workouts. Think about everything you need to do in order to achieve your ultimate dream. Take nutrition; Are you winning at your nutrition each meal? What about each day? Or each week? If you're not winning the week, you can see where your dreams of losing weight are going... down in the dumps.

I recently finished writing out my yearly business goals. I have monthly goals, quarterly goals, and yearly goals. I have number of client goals, money earning goals, starting new venture goals, etc. What I want to acknowledge is that I wrote down all these goals. They are not just in my mind. I have things to aim for. My mindset is to hit these goals, not to come close, but actually hit them or surpass them. If I don't have the mindset to hit these goals that are written down in detail I will most likely never come close to them. Now I *expect* to hit them. I expect to WIN them. And your mindset should be to *expect* to hit your goals. That's a WIN!

Every morning I write my top two or three things that I must get accomplished that day. I usually have ten to twenty things on my mind, but I write down the top two or three and focus on getting those done. When I get those done each day that's a WIN for the day. So, every day I enter the day expecting to win the day.

Having a winning attitude is a decision. It's not something you work towards. A winning attitude takes just a millisecond to get. A non-winning attitude, which is the same as a losing attitude, takes the same amount of time to get. It's up to you to decide which mindset you will have.

A winning attitude becomes easier and easier if you become consistent at it over time. **Focus on small wins each and every day, not winning the year.** By winning each day you'll soon look back over the last year and see that you had a winning mindset eighty to ninety percent of the time.

CHAPTER 14

FEEL BETTER FIRST

DID YOU KNOW THAT FITNESS IS NOT ABOUT HOW FIT YOU ARE? Fitness is really about health. More specifically, how healthy you are. I've been in the health and fitness industry for a long time and have finally figured out from years of watching and listening to clients, mentors, doctors, health professionals, fitness professionals, athletes and more, that the best way to get the health and fitness results you really want is not necessarily to shoot for fitness goals, but to shoot more for being as healthy as possible. You might have smaller goals within that, such as running a marathon, or being able to perform fifteen full push-ups without stopping. But, keep in mind that the more you complete smaller goals such as those I just mentioned, this equals more WINS. This makes you overall healthier. That's what you should really be striving for. Don't set your end goal to lose one hundred pounds. Instead, try losing one hundred pounds to be a healthier, stronger person, mentally and physically.

I have found that the people who focus much more on becoming healthier people are the ones that actually do so. Look at your past family health history and try to reverse something like heart disease that has gone on for generations upon generations. I use that as my example because heart disease is huge in my own family history. It's been a dream of mine to reverse that long standing disease. I want this not only for me, but for my kids as well. My wife and I both push good nutrition, staying hydrated and being physically active with all our kids. You should do the same by setting the example. After all, your kids become who they see. If they see you eating crap most of the week, coming home from work plopping yourself down on the couch every day, being a lazy, non-responsive parents, your kids will most likely become the same type of people. Don't let that happen to our younger generation. Don't let that happen to your own kids. **Set your sights on being as healthy as possible and your percentage of seeing results are much higher than if you just tried to lose one hundred pounds.** A "winning mindset" is better than just a mindset!

CHAPTER 15

BE ACCOUNTABLE TO OTHERS

You've heard it before that it's not a goal unless you write it down. That's a huge part of the accountability factor when having a goal. There's one other part that most people miss. To me, this part is so much more important than just writing it down. What is this part? It's showing someone else what you wrote down. There are hundreds of ways I could tell you how to be accountable to your goals, but let's focus on two parts 1. Writing them down and 2. Showing someone what you wrote, because these are the two things that will take you further than ever before.

1. SEEING IT DAILY WITH "DREAM NOTES"!

Once you know exactly what your goals and dreams are, you must write them down. But where do you write them? The answer is easy. EVERYWHERE! The purpose for writing your goals and dreams down is for you to see them daily. I'm talking everywhere you consistently go, over and over again so it's a constant reminder for you to be thinking about. And I mean constant! Sticky notes can be your

best friend in this situation. I love sticky notes, especially those flo-
rescent colored ones. There's something a little more motivating
when you see your dream written down on a bright lime green or
hot pink sticky note. If your goal is to get off of all your medications,
then write on those sticky notes "NO MORE MEDS!" in big bold letters with a thick marker. Then think of everywhere you consistently
go on a daily basis and put a sticky note in each of those places for
everyone to see. We will talk more about everyone seeing it a bit
later. Put a sticky note on your nightstand so you see it first thing in
the morning right when you wake up and last thing before you head
off to dream land each night. Hopefully you'll be dreaming about
what's written on your sticky note. Put another on your bathroom
mirror so when you're washing your face, brushing your teeth, doing
your hair, you're also seeing that dream of yours. Put another on
the refrigerator door. Better yet, put one inside the fridge so every
time you open it and start to reach for bad food that little sticky note
is looking at you dead in the eyes telling you what you are about
to grab will either hurt or help you reach that goal. Put another in
the pantry where all the dry foods are. Put one on all the TV's in
the house. Put one on your cardiovascular equipment at home; You
know, the treadmill that has all your clothes hanging on it. Put one
on your home computer or keyboard. Put one on your car dashboard.
Put one in your office on your desk. Put one inside the workplace
refrigerator. Put one in a desk drawer so every time you open it you
see that sticky note. You get the point. Put one of your "dream notes"
everywhere you can think of that you consistently go every day. The
point of this is to drive that goal and dream into your head so not a
minute of any day goes by without you thinking about achieving it.
It's a constant reminder of what you really want to achieve. It's not
how to do it, or when to do it, but simply a reminder TO DO IT.

This has been something I have done for most of my life starting with sports. I remember writing down on a white torn piece

of paper written in black marker a note to myself in middle school that simply said "18". I placed that note on a bulletin board where I hung all my track medals, which at that time was just a few. I looked at that "18" note every morning and every night and didn't take it down until I long jumped 18 feet and broke the school record. Guess what? I broke that record with a jump of 18 feet 1/2 in. That's when I finally took that note down. I did the same thing in college, which I'll explain in a minute.

Last year, while coaching the May River High School girls varsity basketball team, our coaching staff and the rest of the girls team came up with team goals, wrote them down in ink on a big white board in the locker room, where the team dressed before every practice and home games. We put season long goals, conference goals, and even game-by-game goals. The point is that we wrote those goals down and every time those girls were in the locker room they saw those goals and the overall season dream that they came up with. Because we did these little things, we had the most amazing season ever, and even ended the season with a nineteen game winning streak until we lost in the final four of the state playoffs. Those goals definitely helped all of us; players and coaches, perform better in each and every game. **Writing down your goals and your overall dream is the main part of success. Without it, you're just going through the motions not really reaching for anything specific. Make sure you do this step and make sure you see it constantly throughout every day.**

Now there is a second part to this... Showing someone what you've wrote. Yes, a goal isn't a goal until you write it down, but that goal you wrote down probably won't happen unless you share it with others. That's called accountability!

While running track in college, I always wrote down my goals for each season just like I did in high school. However, I knew I needed to up my game a little since the competition was a lot better in college than it was in high school. So, I played around with a few ideas of how to share my goals with people. One day after meeting with my psychology professor, we got to talking about how track was going and he wanted to know what my plans were for the season. I told him what my goals were and he said to make those them real. He said I should write those goals down and tape them to my dorm room door on the hallway side. This way when hundreds of people walk by my door every day they all knew what I was trying to achieve. That was eye opening to me. All I was thinking was "What if I don't reach those goals? What will people say if I fail?" He then said that's exactly why I should do it; because it will make me work 110% harder to achieve my dreams. You don't want people to think you failed. And if you do, then you know you gave it your best shot! That was exactly what I needed to hear, so that's exactly what I did. I didn't care what people thought. Maybe they thought I was out of my mind for even reaching for those goals. Maybe they were inspired themselves. It didn't matter to me; it just made me work harder than ever before.

Once you write down your goals and dreams, find someone: a best friend, a spouse, your kids, co- workers, your boss, a teacher, a coach, someone that you trust and show them what you wrote down. Give them a copy to keep. Tell them to keep you accountable. Don't pick people that don't care. Pick people that will build you up and keep you on track. Pick people that will help you achieve your dreams, not nag or laugh at you. It doesn't matter if they think you will or won't achieve what you're striving for. All that matters is that they are there for you when you most need it.

2. WEEKLY MEETINGS.

A good friend and client of mine, Mitch Brown, does what we call an *accountability meeting* with me every Friday at the same time. We simply call each other up to discuss three main topics which I'll talk about in a second. First though, you should know that I know absolutely nothing about his business or industry except that Mitch owns a company called *Boat Float*. Mitch has told me that his company provides environmentally friendly docking and lift solutions for boats. Solutions such as... Lift recommendations and installations, platform lift repairs, topside dock and pier rebuilding, lift removal and relocation, HDPE floating dock design, construction, and installation. (Call Mitch at Boat Float if you need any of these things.)

As I said, I know nothing about his industry and he really knows nothing about mine. However, what we discuss in this *weekly accountability meeting* is 1. Wins, successes, victories that we had over the past week. 2. Obstacles or challenges we had over the week and 3. Goals for the upcoming week. We try to state our top two or three for each topic to stay focused on what really matters. We give each other some advice on any of these topics, and that is that. These calls last from twenty to thirty minutes tops. We keep each other accountable! That is the reason for these calls. We also don't necessarily focus on just business. In fact, when we discuss our weekly WINS, many times it has to do with our families.

My point is that we are holding each other accountable on a weekly basis. Maybe this is something you can do for your health and fitness goals. Find someone that has the same goal as you, or similar, or someone that has gone through and succeeded in what you want to achieve. It can be someone totally different than you. **Find someone you know will stick and stay the course, hold you accountable and keep you motivated. Someone that will push you a little bit. Find someone that will get you a little uncomfortable, meaning hold you accountable to do something that you know needs to be done but are hesitant on doing so. Once you find the right person, schedule a weekly call with them just as Mitch and I do.** It doesn't even have to be a weekly call. Sometimes a monthly call is good, too. I've done monthly calls before, but found that those are harder to stick to. They don't seem to be as important as a weekly call as they usually fall by the wayside. I love doing weekly calls. Getting them scheduled is sometimes hard. Sticking to them and making them happen makes you constantly think about them so it's easier to keep with it.

CHAPTER 16

JOURNALING

JOURNALING IS ANOTHER THING THAT IS VERY POWERFUL. Journaling is something I have always struggled with and am constantly trying to work on because I know the benefits are amazing. For some people journaling comes easy. For others it's very hard and is a struggle to continue doing. You have to at least give it your best try and see how it goes because it is so powerful and can really change your life. The purpose of journaling is to let your mind flow so you open up your dreams. You can hold yourself accountable to things, write down what's bothering you, remember what is going well, and anything and everything you can think of. Just five to ten minutes every morning or at night before you go to bed can make a huge change in your life. I personally like the mornings because my mind is fresh and not thinking about what happened all day long. It's thinking more about what could be, instead of what was.

Journaling can be a game changer and for many it becomes a fantastic habit. Even if you wrote one sentence or phrase each day, or one word per day, this can work wonders. It doesn't have to be a full story, but just a few thoughts. In a sense I do journal myself, but I consider it to be a different form of self-care and growth. As I go over with my accountability partner Mitch, I also write down my victories and failures for the past week, big moments that happened, and goals for the next week on a weekly basis. This is something that I will go into more detail about later in the book.

Something else that I've done in the past and just restarted about six months ago is writing down my THREE MAIN GOALS that need to be accomplished that day as I mentioned in the last chapter. I do this each day either during my breakfast time or as soon as I get into my truck in the early morning before I drive off. I turn on the notes in my smart phone, hit the microphone button and say what the three main things are that I need to get done that day. It's just like writing them down. It becomes "real" by writing them down. So, before the day even begins I have my top three tasks I know I have to accomplish that day. I may say "make a newsletter video" or "go to grocery store" or "stretch for thirty minutes". Whatever my main priorities are to win the day that absolutely need to be accomplished is what I put down.

This is something that can be done for health and fitness purposes. **Write down what the three most important things are that need to be accomplished that day for you to win the day, which will help you win the week, win the month, win the year, and eventually win your dream!**

I know many people who journal daily the same as I mentioned above and go back to see if they won the week. They will journal about their entire week each weekend. They might have won six out of seven days by doing a few big things, then write down how the week went. This is a great idea.

I know others that journal about God or about educational books they are reading. I know people that journal about family and work or just how they feel. There are so many things you can journal about and everyone has their own way to do so. **Find the way that works best for you and stick to it. Don't think about doing it for a year or more. Just start journaling on some type of regular basis, maybe daily or weekly. Just keep it going.** You'll be amazed at how much you'll get out of keeping a consistent journal.

CHAPTER 17

SOCIAL MEDIA

SOCIAL MEDIA IS NOW A VERY LARGE PART OF OUR CULTURE IN today's world and I see this continuing to be the case for quite some time. I'm honestly not a fan of social media because I see a huge loss of the way people communicate. However, I do think it's a great place to market businesses, products and services. It's an awesome way to keep up with old friends and family, and is a fantastic accountability tool for all of us.

I have found friends on social media platforms who I haven't spoken to since middle school, high school or college. I'm able to see if they got married, had kids, where they now work and what hobbies they are into. I think this is great because before social media, I often wondered about this person and that person. I also love social media because my mother who lives in Ohio can see what's happening with our kids. She always wants to know what's going on with her grandkids. She is able to see pictures and see who won games that she wouldn't be able to see otherwise. I can keep track of her, my sister and her family, my aunts and uncles, and cousins. I know a lot about what's going on in their lives just by seeing their posts on Facebook or Instagram.

I also know of so many more businesses, products and services I never knew were out there, all because of social media. I can promote my business for free and that's a wonderful thing because marketing costs a lot these days. If I have an injury and need a great home hand-held massage gun, I can find a great one in seconds. Or, if I want to find a place that designs t-shirts, there are thousands of places all over social media—some local that I didn't even know existed and some that are states away from me.

But the absolute best thing that I have found social media for is *accountability*. Yep! You can easily tell a friend about a goal of yours to have them keep you accountable for it. This is great, and now you can make a post about it and have hundreds, thousands, even millions of people know what your goal is! That's pressure! That will make you work harder than just having one person know about your dream.

Imagine making a post every day of a picture with a towel over your head being a sweaty mess because you just crushed another workout with a hashtag under that picture saying #100poundsdowngoal. And another hashtag saying #goals, or #workingtowardsamarathon, or #selfgrowth, or #keepmeaccountable. This is major accountability without physically telling a soul. This is huge! People will post comments on your post with positive messages telling you how well you are doing. You will also start inspiring others to do the same or to start something for themselves.

However, please don't get in the habit of posting things for "likes". What if Facebook decided to do away with "likes" and comments? Would you still post as much as you do now? Please don't fall in the trap of continually checking how many likes you have or how many people saw your video. To me it's kind of like texting. I'd much rather call and physically talk to someone. It's much more personal and has a real human touch to it. But with social media I apparently have well over one thousand friends, most of whom I don't really know.

Again, social media can be great, but it can also be corrupting as well. **Use social media for accountability partners. Post your goals,** pictures of you doing the little things that will get you there. Post things asking for help. Post things of how well you are doing or even how you failed that day. Use social media for help, but don't get sucked in by looking for "likes" and all that jazz.

CHAPTER 18

ACTIVATING THE PLAN

EVERYONE IS DIFFERENT WHEN IT COMES TO STARTING THE PRO-
cess. Many take this step in various directions, angles, levels, and stages. The main thing is that you *START, or TAKE ACTION.* This means you are no longer just thinking about it. You are no longer just writing it down. You are no longer planning it out.

Taking action means physically doing something today that will change your tomorrow. It's getting up earlier than normal. It's eating a healthy breakfast, starting a workout, going for a walk, reading a book, starting a journal, going to bed earlier, actually getting an accountability partner, posting your dreams on social media, putting sticky notes with your goals on them everywhere you go. These are all physical things that will improve yourself and get you closer to your daily goal, weekly goal, monthly goal, yearly goal, and your main overall dream. The fact is you have to take action! You have to start!

In 2008 through 2010 I was running a lot, training for 5k road races. I ran a lot of them and did fairly well in most. I also was a part of a local running club called the Palmetto Pacers. It was started by Tim Waz, who now owns a running store called Grounded Running, which is located in Beaufort, South Carolina. I joined this running club to meet others who knew more about training for 5k's than I did, even though I had been a cross country coach. You can never stop learning. So after about two years of running A LOT of 5k's I decided to run some longer races: 8k's, 10k's, and eventually half marathons. These were very difficult for me because I'm a former sprinter and long jumper; I am no distance runner by any means. I really had no idea how to train for these things. I got through these distances with some hard work, but then I made up my mind to finally run a full marathon. This was completely out of my league, especially when it came to training for it. I signed up to run the Rock and Roll Marathon, the first in Savannah, Georgia in November 2011. I knew I needed help, so I asked Tim how to train for something like this. I'll always remember his answer. He simply said to "Start." It was the simplest answer and the answer that I needed to hear, because I was thinking I needed to first sit down, come up with this elaborate plan way before I actually did any training. Well I was completely wrong. Until then, I hadn't really trained more than ten miles at a time for anything. That day Tim made me run a grueling twelve-mile loop around the town of Bluffton. I thought I was going to die, especially when he made me sprint it in during the last half mile.

I was dead as a doornail after that run. It was much worse than the one half marathon I ran a few months earlier. This dude took me to another level when I didn't think I had one on a very hot and humid day. But, he made me "start." He made me get into action right away and I thank him for that. I did come up with a full training schedule and plan shortly after. It was five months-worth of training before the big race and it was perfect. I ran that Rock and Roll Marathon, and finished. I was more than happy with my whole training plan and glad that I started the way I did, with Tim trying to kill me on day one. It was exactly what I needed.

There are a few things I suggest getting started with right now on a daily basis that will help you attain your health and fitness goals. I don't know exactly what your goals are in health and fitness, but I do know that if you do these things I'm about to go over, and take action on these now, it will help get you a lot closer to your goals. Try them out.

1. ***Start a regular AM routine.*** I absolutely LOVE getting up before the sun and seeing the sunrise. You will find more sunrise pictures on my social media posts than anything else. It's just something that drives me. Watching the sun come up with all the different colors and patterns in the sky is calming and puts your mind at peace with the world. Getting up early is not for everyone, but I highly suggest doing it as you will get more done in the early morning hours than any other time of the day. This is when your mind is fresh and ready to work.

My morning routine is waking up with my 5:00AM alarm. I'd say six out of seven days I wake up on my own before my alarm. It's just habit after doing it for thirty years. I get up right away, head to the bathroom where I already have clothes laid out from the night before, get dressed, splash cold water on my face, brush my teeth, all in about ten minutes. Let's talk about that cold water on the face for a moment. Either splash cold water on your face or take a warm shower and make it really cold for about thirty seconds right before you turn it off. The reason for this is to wake the body. It changes the body core temperature and gets the heart pumping a bit, which wakes you up, physically and mentally. It's a great practice to get into. I then head to the kitchen to get a healthy breakfast; Something full of energy so I feel awake and have a great mindset for the day ahead. While I'm eating, I'll pull out my smart phone and put in my notes the top three things that I need to get accomplished that day (sometimes I wait until I get into my truck on the way to work). I've been doing this for some time now and it really keeps me focused on what really matters that day. Once I'm done eating, I get on the road for a ten to fifteen minute ride to my Cannonfit studio. While driving

I will put on one of three things; an educational book on Audible (sometimes I go spiritual and listen to bible verses), a podcast or inspirational YouTube videos or speeches. This short ride to work gets me pumped up and in the best mindset I possibly can be before my first clients start walking in at 5:55AM. Sometimes, depending how early I wake up, I might get to the studio about ten minutes before everyone else and I'll do some ladder drills, and the old sprint drills I did during my track days. This gets my heart rate up, adrenaline going and endorphins pumping! If I were to walk into work in the morning with everyone else and I say "Oh man I'm tired today", I'd be doing a disservice to my clients. I have to be inspirational, motivational and inspiring the moment people walk in. Then I pump up the volume on some fast beat music like the Rocky theme, Imagine Dragons, ACDC, The Who, Eminem, or some head bopping hip hop and be as enthusiastic as I can to motivate everyone else. This goes on for hours. I always take a small break for forty five minutes starting at 9:00AM for my own strength workout, HIIT training, cardio or stretching. Then it's back to training clients again at 9:45AM until about 1:00PM. That's my morning routine most days.

Now on the weekends, I'll still get up early. I try to get one extra hour of sleep, but it hardly ever happens. I'll get up, get dressed, eat breakfast just like during the week, but on Saturdays I write for at least an hour. If I'm not writing, I'm reading. Then I'll go for a long two to three mile nature walk. I walk to the Parkside in our neighborhood where there is a huge pond and grassy area with a gazebo in the middle. There are always a few alligators laying on the side of the pond and birds flying around. I love watching the sunrise over that pond. It's truly amazing! I walk around the whole thing a couple of times listening to either a book, a podcast or scripture. This is my once per week ME TIME. Every now and then I won't listen to anything but nature. It's so calming and I need that time to recoup and get refreshed. After my walks, I usually lay on the floor, still with my ear pods in, listening to whatever I was zoned in on during my walk and stretch for thirty to forty minutes. At first this was hard. I try to stretch for twenty to thirty minutes daily now, but time does get in the way a lot. Once I started this stretching routine, which is the same every time I do it, my body started feeling better. It's truly an amazing feeling when you open up the hips, relax the muscles, and let the blood flow.

On Sundays I get up early, eat breakfast and start on my weekly online coaching. I like to get this done while everyone else is still sleeping. Then I might get about thirty minutes of interval cardio in, burning four to five hundred calories on my home elliptical or spin bike, then shower and church.

I suggest you get an AM routine that works best for you. Everyone is different so what works for me might not work well for you. Whatever routine you come up with, make sure it has a healthy breakfast for energy, something to get your mindset ready for the day, something that will educate, motivate and inspire you, and lastly something that gets your endorphins flowing through your body to get the blood moving and groovin'!

2. *Eat a great breakfast*. Eating a great breakfast has many options. I live down South in what we call the low country and people that grew up here love to have a fully cooked hot breakfast like eggs, sausage, hash-browns, grits and gumbo just to name a few. That is certainly NOT me! This is one reason why over half of America is overweight. Let's make this simple. You need some energy and that comes from most foods that are high in fiber like whole wheat toast, english muffins, or oatmeal. You need some protein for fat burning like yogurt or eggs. You need some good veggies or fruit for essential nutrients, vitamins and minerals. And you need a good glass of water or a drink that will give you energy. I say the word "energy" meaning something that will make you feel good, not put you into overdrive and something that has tons of sugar in it. I do recommend

caffeine as it is a great way to get the body awake and feeling good so your body is ready to move and perform better right away. I personally have a healthy drink every morning called Zeal+ from Zurvita. It's full of vitamins and nutrients and has some caffeine also. It's not loaded with sugar like most energy drinks are and it really gets my mind feeling at 100% right away without the super high burst of energy. Instead I feel refreshed with a clear mind. You can go to my studio website at www.cannonfit.com to find a link for Zeal+. Make breakfast be a great meal as it will get your mind and body working at its best right away. We all need that.

3. *Read or listen to a book, podcast, or YouTube video* for ten to fifteen minutes before your day begins. This is something I have done for years. I started with turning on YouTube motivational videos and listening to them while eating breakfast and driving to work. Then I slowly added some podcasts to my routine, and now sometimes it's a book on Audible. I highly recommend Audible as well as real books and Audible lets you listen to books, and podcasts at a faster pace so you can get them done faster and learn more. I like to have a real book at night and listen to books all other times of the day as my time is limited. I have to say this: I have probably listened to enough podcasts and books in the last year to earn me a master's degree in two different subjects. How many people can say that? I have learned more from books and podcasts in the last year than I probably did from my own four-year college degree. That's not a cut on the college I attended. I'm just saying I have learned a lot in the last year. I can't get enough! My wish list on Audible has so many books in it that it would probably take me four or five years to finish them all. Imagine what you can do with all the knowledge you might learn from doing this step on a daily basis for the next year. The knowledge you gain from this is endless.

4. *Eat your greens.* My wife makes this great green drink that she picked up from someone else. It's a "cleansing" drink, but really, it's

just a healthy green drink full of vitamins and nutrients that helps the digestive system work a lot better. It's loaded with things like celery, kale, spinach, green apple, and a bunch of other stuff. Honestly, I don't even ask what's in it, but I know that I love it! It tastes amazing. There are a million versions of green drinks out there that you could start having daily. And if you don't add them together for a smoothie type drink, make sure you eat plenty of greens throughout the day. Greens are so rich in vitamins and nutrients that your body absolutely needs. If you eat these on a consistent basis you body will thank you. Your digestive system will also thank you. You'll start to trim down because of the better digestion. You'll start having more energy from all the vitamins, minerals and nutrients. There are so many benefits from greens that help the body that it's almost unbelievable. Get your greens in!

5. *Refuel your metabolism every three hours* with good nutritious foods. This is always a hot topic. I want to make this as simple as possible because that's how you should see it as... simple. Breakfast, which I already spoke about, I believe is your most important meal. It should be a great meal to amp up the metabolism and get the body going. After that just make sure to *refuel* the metabolism every three hours with three main things. A protein for fat burning, a complex carbohydrate for energy and a fruit or vegetable for overall wellness. Keeping the metabolism refueled is the main thing. That's key for fat loss and keeping energy levels high, not feeling sluggish, not having an energy crash in the middle of the day, keeping muscles strong and most importantly, keeping your mind right. What your personal eating patterns are and how you eat completely effects how your brain works. If you keep your nutrition strong, you keep your mind strong.

6. *Drink lots of water.* My wife and I are constantly on our kids about drinking water. I mean constantly! They just don't realize how much water the body needs and how water makes you feel better. And, honestly, most adults aren't any better. In fact, adults are probably

worse. My college track coach, Bob Willey, a very wise man, always said to never pass a water fountain without taking a drink. To this day I have never forgotten that. Drinking water helps your energy, keeps the metabolism revved up, and keeps the body hydrated enough to keep going with sports and everyday performance as well as keeps the mind sharp and focused. Try drinking more water and cutting out all the sugary drinks that only make the body sluggish and weak. I suggest to simply carry a water bottle around with you all day long, everywhere you go. You go to the bathroom; the bottle goes with you. You go to the copy machine; the bottle goes with you. It never leaves your side. When the water runs out, just refill it. People just don't get enough water in their bodies and we as a whole must do a better job at staying hydrated instead of only hydrating every time we get dehydrated. A simple rule of thumb is to drink about half your body weight in ounces each day.

7. *Get seven to eight hours of sleep*. I cannot begin to explain how important this step is. Getting the proper amount of rest your body needs each day is huge when it comes to the metabolism running correctly, keeping your brain activity high, you losing or gaining weight, how your body feels, headaches, dehydration, depression, daily function and performance, muscle recovery and rejuvenation, and so much more. Try to get at least seven hours of sleep during the work week and possibly eight hours on the weekends. This means you have to plan ahead. If you know you have to wake up at 5:00AM, you must be asleep at 10:00PM. Simply count backwards seven hours. Make yourself go to sleep earlier.

8. *Journal and write down weekly wins, losses, challenges, and goals for the next week*. I spoke about this earlier in the book, but let me mention it again here. This strategy really helps to get organized, and more focused. If there is a lack of organization and focus while training to attain a health and fitness goal, or any goal of any type for that matter, you may as well kiss that dream goodbye. Getting

organized and staying focused is the consistency part of attaining goals. Keeping a journal will help with this. I love to write down my weekly wins, meaning two or three great things that happened that week. I also write down two or three losses, meaning things that got me off track or things that I'm disappointed about. With this I write the main challenges that I encountered over the past week. Things that might have held me back from accomplishing something important. And lastly, I will write the two or three main goals I want or need to accomplish the next week. This can easily be a journal. Writing down every morning the two or three main things that needs to be accomplished that day is also great. Writing down monthly goals, quarterly goals, or yearly goals are great too. Even just putting down on paper one sentence about how the day went. Doing this really gets the mind right and keeps the mind focused and on task. If done consistently it's a total game changer!

CHAPTER 19

DON'T SKIP. CONSISTENCY IS THE ONLY WAY TO WIN!

I JUST SPOKE A LITTLE BIT ABOUT CONSISTENCY. YOU CAN HONESTLY take the word consistency and put it on any topic in the world and get better results. That's how much consistency means when it comes to reaching any health and fitness goal.

We all have issues. I certainly do! We all go out of town every now and then. I do this, too. We all have family or friends come stay with us at times. Yes, this happens to me as well. Does this give you an out of your goals and dreams? It shouldn't. These are just obstacles. That's all. Plan for them ahead of time and stay consistent. If you take a trip to Disney World in the middle of your hundred-pound weight loss journey. Should this completely derail the whole dream? NO! Plan ahead. Keep up with your journaling. Keep up with your workouts with push-ups, squats, lunges, crunches, dips and planks in the smallest five foot area of a hotel room. Keep eating your protein, complex carb and fruit or veggies every three hours. Keep up with your cardio by walking or going for a short run around the hotel before heading to one of the parks. Yes, go ahead and have some deserts and different foods you don't normally have. If you mess up it's not a deal breaker—just get back on track the next day. It's not a big deal in the long haul. It was just one day; Or maybe it was four days. Four days during a dream that you have planned on taking a year to achieve won't kill you. Just get back to it. Stop worrying about one or two bad days and just get back on track again the next day.

Think about if you ate really well; what you ate, when you ate, and how much you ate, for six days each week. But each week you also had one terrible day. Over a one year long haul each week eating great six days out of each week and eating terribly just one day out of each week, how does that year look? I'll tell you. That's three hundred twelve really good days and only fifty two bad days. I'm confident if you did that over a year your results would be tremendous! So, don't sweat the small stuff, because that's all this is—small stuff.

Now if you want faster results, just don't skip— Ever! My clients come to me saying "I'm going on vacation next week; can I make up those sessions when I get back?". "Sure," I say, "but you'll lose some real good consistency in the process." I'd rather send them workouts to do, even if those workouts only take ten minutes. It's the consistency that matters more. So, if you normally strength train on Mondays, Wednesdays and Fridays, your goal is to stay as consistent as possible with only doing strength training on those days each week. If you also do cardio on Tuesdays, Thursdays and Saturdays, and skip one to make up another, you are now throwing off your consistency routine. This does affect your results. The more consistent you are, the better and faster results you will have.

In college, Coach Willey planned out our training schedule before the season even started so we would peak, or be at our best on Fridays and Saturdays. Those are the days we competed during the season. We had to have fresh legs as track athletes say, on competition days. Our hardest days each week were always during the beginning of the week. Let's say I had a sore knee, or something just didn't feel right so I took one of those hard training days off. It wouldn't be very smart of me to make up that workout by doing it on Thursday or Friday because my legs would feel heavy and sluggish, with not enough recovery, and I would run much slower or jump a lot shorter than I would have while competing if I just would have followed the weekly plan and tapered throughout the week. Even though we were a NAIA school, we also competed with NCAA Division I schools, which I loved. I thrived on that. And if I didn't follow the plan, I knew I was toast. I wanted to be as fresh as I could be each track meet, so I made sure to follow Coach Willey's workouts. And guess what? When you follow a plan, be consistent, and never skip, things go pretty well in the end!

One of my mantra's today is "Never Skip Mondays." But when it comes to your workout, don't miss Mondays, EVER! This is how you start your week; Don't start it off with skipping your workout. Over the past thirty years as a fitness coach I have found that the day of the week that most people cancel, reschedule or completely skip is Monday. Be consistent every Monday and start your week off feeling great!

Another tip I saw recently from Dwayne "The Rock" Johnson was to get just a little bit of exercise in every Sunday. Just a little sweat, not a full-blown workout. I've done this before with work stuff, but never really thought about doing the same with exercise. I do take a walk every Sunday, so it's kind of the same. By getting a good sweat in on the days you usually don't do any type of intentional workout you'll burn more calories that might make a HUGE difference over the long hull.

Being consistent is the key to everything when it comes to getting results. **You can start doing everything in this book for one month and get better, but if you stop after one month nothing really changed. Be consistent and get results!**

CHAPTER 20

HAVING A SHORT-TERM MEMORY

While going through the process towards your goal(s) it is important for your mindset to have a short-term memory. Jay Bilas, a former Duke Basketball player talked about in his book Toughness, how Coach Mike Krzyzewski, the well-known Head Men's Basketball Coach at Duke University has always preached to his players the importance of having a short-term memory. Coach K insists that to be totally focused throughout entire practices, games and seasons, every player must forget about what just happened and look forward to what's next. If a player took a shot and missed, he wants them to forget about it and move on because they cannot do anything about it, especially if it were a good shot. Even if a player made a great shot, stole the ball, or did something amazing to help the team, Coach K tells them to forget about that and look to what's next. Otherwise you might get beat down the floor while celebrating what you just accomplished.

Basketball is a game of continuous up and down the floor, non-stop running, always moving from offense to defense and back again. Players don't have time to stop and think, or stop and be mad at themselves for missing an open shot or throwing a bad pass because their opponent will be up the floor scoring a basket while they are still shaking their head being mad at themselves. Instead, the "what's next" mentality keeps players focused and mentally in the game. This also makes players tougher. I'm talking about being mentally tougher and focused.

This is also true when it comes to your process of transforming your body. Let's say you do a great job for two full weeks, doing everything to the best of your ability; eating correctly, never missing a workout, working on your mindset, keeping accountable to and from others, and so on. Then one day you crash and burn pretty hard, totally missing on just one single part of the process like your nutrition. After you messed up and ate terribly that day, are you going to fret about it and focus on those bad things while you could be moving on from it, or are you going to actually move on from it and look to what's next? Just because you mess up on one thing doesn't mean you've messed up on achieving your overall goal.

Things are going to happen as I discussed before with knowing that obstacles will come up. It's how you deal with those obstacles that makes or breaks you achieving your dream. Staying focused on your overall dream, your overall goal is all about being in the present, not what just happened and certainly not what might happen later. Being focused on "what's next", meaning the very next thing you can do to improve your outcome, will determine if you will be successful or not.

Work on having that short-term **memory and forget about what just happened, good or bad, or even what happened a long time ago, because you cannot go back and fix it. Instead, try to only think of the absolute next thing that can be done. The thing that you need to focus on to be successful.**

CHAPTER 21

NUTRITION—IS THIS REALLY THAT IMPORTANT?

THAT IS AN EASY ANSWER... HECK YES, MORE THAN YOU CAN POS-sibly imagine. There are certain things that absolutely must change for people to have any kind of transformation success when it has to do with health and fitness. First and foremost is *mindset*. That must be changed. If you don't change the way you think, then you'll end up back to where you started, or even worse. The second thing is *nutrition*. I could write an entire book just on nutrition and all the different ways it effects the body. But I'll try to keep this topic to a couple pages since I want to make this simple to understand and easy for you and most people to make the changes needed to see the individual results to be successful.

When it comes to thinking about nutrition most people start freaking out because there is so much information out there, a lot good, and even more not so good. Let's get down to the nitty gritty and make this as simple as possible for you. However, I need to make it clear that not everyone reading this book has the same goal. Not everyone needs or wants to lose weight. But, most people do need to lose fat. Wait... what? Losing weight and losing fat are two totally different things and you need to understand that. I'm going to tell you a story that I tell many of my clients. I'm going to tell you are true story about me that might help you understand.

In 2011 I decided to run a marathon, the same marathon I talked about earlier in the book. I was in phenomenal shape and felt amazing. My strength was good, my nutrition was very good, and my lung capacity was good and getting even better with the training. I weighed 155 lbs when I started training five months before the race and my body fat was down to 12%, which is very good. This is important so don't forget that.

When I started training for this marathon in May 2011 my training consisted of running just four days per week and strength training three days per week. My running consisted of;

- Mondays: Three—four miles comfortably. Total body strength training routine
- Tuesdays: Longer interval runs—half mile run faster than my intended race pace with a quarter mile walk rest four—six times
- Wednesdays: Total body strength training
- Thursdays: Shorter, faster intervals such as four hundred to six hundred meters with shorter rests
- Fridays: Strength training days and longer comfortable runs from six—eight miles
- Saturdays: Rest days
- Sundays: Long run days starting with ten miles and increasing that every two to three weeks.

As each week came my long runs got a little longer, the intervals got a little more, and the long, long run days became long. About halfway through my training, around the third month I started to run out of training time because everything was getting longer and taking up more time, plus I was working more than full time hours, as most trainers do. Therefore, I had to make a decision to create either more time in the day, which wasn't an option, or cut something in my training. I had to cut the strength training to one day per week and keep doing some preventative exercises for my legs after my longer runs such as toe raises, heel raises, side leg raises and bridges. That was about it. By the time the last month of training came around I had completely stopped all major strength training because of time and because I needed more recovery time.

So trying to make this long story shorter, the day I ran the marathon, I was in great marathon shape, meaning my lungs could go on forever and ever. However, I felt sluggish, weak, and skinny. I dropped ten full pounds weighing 145 lbs, which most people would be thrilled about. Not me—I remember checking my body fat the day before the race and it was an amazing 25%. I was now 25% fat when I was just 12% fat five months earlier. And I trained my butt off, literally. How is that possible, especially when I lost 10 lbs? I felt like crap, and looked like crap. But man oh man, I could run a marathon with no problem.

You see muscle weighs a lot more than fat. And since I cut out most of my strength training, I lost a whole lot of my muscle: apparently 10 lbs worth. So, I lost weight, but got A LOT fatter, plus felt and looked terrible. When people tell me they want to lose weight, I usually come back and say, "you mean you want to lose fat?". Then I'll tell them my story. There is a big difference in losing weight and losing fat. Once you get it in your head that it's fat that you want and need to lose, you'll be in a better mindset, and your process will be easier. Plus, you won't have to run a marathon to do it! Ha Ha! Not that running a marathon was a bad thing; It was awesome and I'll never take it back. I needed to run it as I was apparently going through a mid- life crises, needing to prove to myself that I was still "da man"! Needless to say, I gained back the muscle weight and got my body fat back down with some hard strength training and good nutrition.

Now back to nutrition. Everyone, almost, needs to lose fat: Body builders. The goal for them is to be as lean as possible, meaning have the least amount of fat on them during their competition. The same goes for you and me. We want to be as lean as possible. What that really means is the more muscle you have, the less fat you have because you burn fat through muscle. This does not mean you have to become a body builder to do so. The difference in body builders and you and me is the amount of calories they consume. Body builders take in 5,000-10,000 calories each day. Most of that is chicken, fish or some sort of protein. For the average person wanting to lose weight, meaning losing more fat, the usual amount of calories to take in is around 1,500 to 2,500 per day depending on the individual. So, the fact is we want to add as much muscle as we can to burn more fat. It's not necessarily the weight we want to be, it's really the body fat percentage we want to be. Remember I lost 10 lbs during that marathon training, but gained 15% more fat. I also felt and looked terrible. This should tell you one thing right now; You need to do some sort of strength training.

What does this have to do with nutrition you ask? Well, you can think of nutrition just like strength training. This is about as simple as I can put this...

1. Eating protein helps the body build more muscle, which equals more fat burning.
2. Eating complex carbohydrates help give the body the energy needed to sustain life, to do your everyday activities, keeps the metabolism running at a faster rate and helps add any extra physical activity you choose to do, like working out.
3. Eating fruits and vegetables helps the wellness side of the body needed to live from vitamins, minerals and nutrients. This is what keep us healthy.

Now that you understand that different types of foods help the body do completely different things and causes the body to react differently, it's easy to see that it is very essential to have all three components each time you eat. However, I'm not going to get into what proteins are and what complex carbohydrates are. You can easily google that and come up with a list of foods that you can choose from. That takes about five minutes and I highly suggest doing so.

What I really want to tell you is how to put it all together. This is where it gets fun, so let's start at the very beginning.

Breakfast—One of the first things I learned in graduate school at Marshall University (Go Herd!) was all about the metabolism. Did you know that the metabolism starts to slow down about every three hours? Therefore, we must fuel that metabolism before it starts the slowing down process. I took that to another level in the year 1999. I was living in Savannah, Georgia working as a fitness director at a big box gym. I decided to put myself through some nutrition tests. I was young and dumb, I know, but I was curious to see what my own body would do. So, for two months I tested out my metabolism. I figured if three hours was the mark that the metabolism started slowing down, I'd try eating every two hours throughout the day. I also figured I'd get the least amount of time between my last meal of the day and the first meal the next day. I knew sleep was important, so I didn't wake up at night to eat. I ate my breakfast within thirty minutes of waking up, not when I got up, but from when I woke up. I probably ate before that thirty minutes but never waited longer than that. I then refueled my metabolism every two hours throughout the day with the proper amount of calories needed (I'll get into that later) up until the moment I went to bed. I ate all the proper things and stayed around my daily calorie range that I needed. I had great results.

I then tried doing the same things but refueling every hour on the nose, still staying around my daily calorie intake. I did this again for two months. I thought my results would be even better, but they actually weren't. I gained a few pounds. I then tried every three hours and after two months of that had amazing results. I didn't keep a log of anything unfortunately. I sure wish I would have, but I remember being very strict on myself. I also remember that the eating every hour test was hard. Not so much the eating part, but the planning part, and always having food with me and eating when I didn't have time. That was difficult.

I have always eaten my breakfast within thirty minutes of waking up to rev-up the metabolism, which in turn gets the body feeling better sooner than later in many different areas, not just the metabolism, but also the mind. Your brain seems to wake up and your thought process seems to be better, as well as your energy level getting higher much faster when eating sooner.

I have also continued to eat something late at night staying on the three-hour refueling times. If I'm going to bed at 10:00PM and my three-hour refueling clock is over at 9:00PM I'll eat again. I've done this for twenty years now and if you look at my picture on the back of this book, it doesn't look like I've gained any major weight.

My rule of thumb is to get the metabolism started and revved up right away each day no more than thirty minutes after waking up. I know a lot of people that don't eat breakfast at all. I'm not sure how they even function. I wonder how much better they could be feeling just by adding this one meal. I dread those days when I have to fast before having blood work done. I end up feeling like a pile of doo doo and my whole day is shot! That's how much it affects me so I know **if you're one of those people that don't eat breakfast and you started eating it, you will start to feel amazing. It will take time but within two weeks of consistently revving up your metabolism right when you wake up, I promise you'll feel like a million bucks!**

Now let's talk about refueling the metabolism every three hours. A fast metabolism is what you really want. If you focus all the time just on weight loss or even fat loss, just thinking day after day about how much you lost that day, it gets stressful. When there is a lot of mental stress, the less likely your body changes. You certainly don't want that. So **instead of constantly trying to lose weight or body fat, just try to focus on everything you can do to increase the metabolism.** Increasing things always seems easier mentally.

I want you to think of your metabolism as a wood burning fire. Imagine you have a small flame going and you add two logs over that flame. Soon that small flame will be a big, beautiful, very hot fire. If the flame is your metabolism and the logs are the food, you eat this now begins to make sense. Sooner or later that big fire goes down as the two logs are now burnt to a crisp, just like the metabolism does in the body. This is the time to add a little more wood to the fire, or a little more food to the body to keep the metabolism going. It's not so much eating every three hours, but refueling the body every three hours. To make it simple on you just **try to never go over the** three-hour **mark without refueling again.** If done consistently over time you will know when the three-hour mark hits as your body will tell you. You'll start to get sluggish, tired, weak, cranky and less focused; That's when you need to refuel. If you do happen to go well past your refueling time, a different energy system in your body has kicked in. We don't really want this to happen. If this happens, you'll sometimes not feel hungry anymore, so you won't eat, thus slowing down the metabolism. And that defeats the whole purpose. Remember the whole point is to keep the metabolism as fast as possible, so slowing it down will only set you back.

I know what you're thinking. "This sounds like a whole lot of food". It does sound like that, but it's not. **A simple way to figure all this out is using www.calculator.net to figure out how many calories to intake per day you'll need to get results. As an example, let's say that this calculator tells you to eat around 1800 calories per day, and you know you are going be awake for seventeen hours. That means you should eat at least six times that day because you** should refuel every three hours. Now divide 1800 calories by six hours. That tells you that you should eat 300 calories each time you eat. Now take that 300 calories and break that up into three parts (about 50% protein, 25% complex carb, 25% fruit or vegetable). Maybe you have grilled chicken for your protein, brown rice for your complex carb, and green beans for your veggie. Take about a half of a chicken breast, a small palmful of brown rice and a small palmful of green beans. Don't forget your water! That doesn't seem like much food now, does it? In fact, you will probably be hungry before the next three hours hits, which is great.

Once you do this just once, you will know about how much your serving sizes should be. After that just estimate it. If you keep measuring food day after day you will eventually stop doing it and fall off the wagon completely. I don't recommend counting calories or measuring your foods all the time. Once you do it once you basically know about how much is correct. This is easy to do.

Here's a great hint: If you are hungry all the time your metabolism is running fast. If you are not that hungry, this means your metabolism is probably slower than it should be.

There are simple things you can do to help the eating process. On Sundays try coming up with a list of what you will be eating on a daily basis for each meal/snack. Then go to the grocery store and get everything you'll need for the week. By the time Mondays come around you'll have the food for each meal throughout the day, every day. Plan it out, then go shopping for it. Make it even easier by cooking a lot of it on Sundays. Put small portions in smaller containers for two or three days so all you have to do is heat it up if needed. Also, always carry a cooler with you to store and have all that food with you at all times.

CHAPTER 22

EXERCISE DOESN'T HAVE TO BE HARD

EXERCISE, THE THING EVERYONE TURNS TO FIRST WHEN THEY want to lose weight. It's the one thing that is easiest to add into your everyday life. It's much easier than changing your diet. It's a whole lot easier than changing your mindset. Just start exercising. That's what happens every January 1st. People flock to the gym for hours upon hours, joining for a year or more at a discounted rate, only to find out that spending two hours on a treadmill every day for one week made them gain weight. Once this happens these people stop going to the gym all together, but keep on paying for that one or two year membership. It happens every year all around the planet, especially in the U.S.

What these people didn't know was while hopping on a treadmill seems like the easiest and smartest way to lose weight, it's actually the last step in the process. There are a few things that people need to change first:

1.   Mindset. If you aren't ready to make a change, you will not make any changes. This means changing the way you think: about

foods, about sleep, about educating yourself, about goal setting, about daily habits—all before you start to exercise.

2.   Nutrition. Most people can completely change their body image just by changing the way they eat (but remember strength training is still needed). Strength training only helps the nutrition part better. But, once the mindset is changed and nutritional habits have been changed, then it is time to think about exercise. So let me dig into that a little bit.

The real question is how do you get the most out of exercise? How will working out help you look better, feel better and perform better? And how do you know what type of exercise or exercise program is right for you? After all there are so many forms of exercise out there. How do you know which is best for you and your results? There is cardiovascular exercise: like walking, jogging, biking, playing basketball, tennis, getting on an elliptical or Peloton, joining a spin class, rowing class, and more. There are also cardiovascular classes with some strength training added like boot camps, Orange Theory, Pure Barr classes, and mommy and me classes. Then you have classes like Yoga classes, Pilates, boxing classes. Then there's always online training/coaching, fitness apps galore, hiring an in-person coach, joining a big box gym, or a personal training studio. And of course, don't forget about at-home training, doing it all on your own or following YouTube videos.

There are so many options out there that sometimes it's just hard to figure out where to even get started. The goal is not to make exercise so hard that you don't want to do it. Many times people think that exercise is supposed to be hard. That is not the case at all. In the next three chapters let me give you a few basics that everyone should have in their exercise routine. Then you can figure out how you want to incorporate those into your exercise routine. But, before I get to those you should know the three main parts of exercise that I believe should always be incorporated; mobility (function through a full range of motion), force production (resistance training), and metabolic conditioning (cardiovascular training).

The first part is **mobility.** This is very often the most overlooked part and probably the most critical part as well, especially as we get older. I, myself have been the one who has lived and learned about neglecting mobility and putting the next two parts first. Trust me when I say that mobility most definitely comes first before any other part, when it comes to sport performance, or just everyday activities and living a pain-free life.

Mobility is moving the body in multiple directions, in a full range of motion. Mobility gives you the ability to perform the five fundamental movements and allows you to control your body throughout those movements.

The five fundamental movements: 1. squatting and hinging 2. lunging 3. pushing 4. pulling and 5. rotating.

Having good mobility slows down the effects of the aging process, and that is what we all want. Having proper mobility makes sure the muscles are lengthened and shortened the way they were designed to. Mobility also improves connective tissue and muscle strength to minimize the risk of injuries, as well as enhances body awareness and balance. Falling is always an issue even at forty or fifty years old. Balance and coordination can get better as we get older, so adding this into your routine is crucial. Lastly, mobility can help in active recovery. We still want to exercise hard, pushing ourselves to new levels instead of maintaining what we have. Doing a mobility workout right after or the day after hard workouts will help recovery and maintain a youthful fitness level that we all strive for.

The second part is **force production with exercise.** There are two types of force production; strength and power. These two help the muscles produce more force more efficiently. Strength is basically the amount of weight that muscles can lift. Power is the velocity of force production, or the speed that creates more force.

The third part is *metabolic conditioning* . These are your energy sources. We have the aerobic oxidative, which uses fat and oxygen to produce energy. Then there is the aerobic glycolytic, which uses oxygen and carbohydrates to produce energy. The anaerobic glycolytic that uses carbohydrates without oxygen to produce energy. And lastly there is stored ATP.

By adding all four of these metabolic conditioning parts together you'll have a great HIIT workout that I will talk more about in chapter 24. HIIT Training is very beneficial if done two-three times per week. HIIT Training increases energy metabolism, meaning it helps the body get rid of unwanted energy and body weight. HIIT Training also helps BDNF (brain derived neurotrophic factor). This is a protein that helps you grow new brain cells and keeps your brain sharp and functioning well.

All this seems pretty complicated and honestly it is and I've probably lost you a bit in the chapter, so let me break it down in a way that seems a lot easier and less confusing in the next few chapters.

While mindset and nutrition are key factors, make sure that you also add in to every routine *mobility, force production and metabolic conditioning.*

CHAPTER 23

WE ALL NEED SOME SORT OF RESISTANCE TRAINING

I'M SKIPPING OVER MOBILITY TRAINING FOR A MOMENT, BUT I WILL come back to it I promise. I want to discuss what people know a little bit about first. Resistance training.

There are so many types of resistance training it's hard to pick just one. So don't! Variation is great when it comes to working out the body. Strength training machines, free weights, bands, body weight, kettlebells and cable machines are a few that many people know about. These can all be used for resistance training, or strength training as some might call it. Resistance training is the form of exercise that burns the most fat. Remember that when next January comes around and you see everyone rush to the gym on New Year's day and jump on a piece of cardio equipment like a treadmill or elliptical for an hour or two then go home. Resistance training burns more fat, not an hour or two of cardio.

Most people avoid the resistance training part because it hurts: Meaning they get sore. Many people don't like that feeling of being sore, yet there are also many people that crave it, like me and most people that workout quite often. These people realize the good it's doing, and realize that it's always a short term soreness. Sometimes there isn't any soreness at all.

Let's discuss muscle soreness for a bit. When we workout with some sort of resistance training, we are putting our muscles at stress, on purpose. When this happens our muscle fibers actually stretch and pull apart just a little, not completely apart. At that point we should actively rest and recover those particular muscle groups that are sore for a day or two. Those muscles then get stronger. We feel the soreness because the muscles fibers are actually being stretched apart. And this is what's supposed to happen. The soreness always goes away. Plus, once you understand that it's just soreness, not pain, you'll truly understand the point of it.

However, you shouldn't feel muscle soreness all the time. Being sore is not the goal! It is good to be sore once in a while like once a week or once every two weeks, but certainly not all the time. It's good to overload the muscles once or twice a month. This means to do more resistance or weight than you previously have. You are pushing the limits of the muscle. Again, just a few times each month. I personally like doing this every two weeks with each body part. There are many different ways to accomplish this as I will discuss later on. When you aren't overloading the muscles, you should be maintaining muscle strength. This is when you are not sore the next day.

When it comes to resistance training there are different ways to format a good program. For fat loss purposes I personally love working the entire body each time I do strength training. There are also many people that like to break up different body parts each day, such as back and biceps on Mondays, legs and shoulders on Tuesdays and so on. Most body builders do this type of thing. I have done that also. But when it comes to those that really want and need to lose a lot of weight and fat, I love total body strength training three days per week. Over my thirty years of coaching people, this has by far been the best for getting results. If done in a combination with cardiovascular training, which I'll talk more about in the next chapter.

There are main muscle groups that you will want to work on:

UPPER BODY—BACK, CHEST, SHOULDERS, TRICEPS AND BICEPS.

That's keeping it simple as there are different muscle groups within each of those areas, but just keep it simple.

LOWER BODY—QUADRICEPS, HAMSTRINGS, GLUTEALS.

Again, there are different muscle groups within these areas, but no need to be obsessed with them unless you're planning to go on stage or train for a specific sport.

It's simple to come up with exercises for each of these muscle groups. Just type in "back exercises" on YouTube and you'll have access to millions of videos on exercises for the back. I have a few hundred on the CannonFit YouTube page as well.

I will get into how to format these exercises all together in just a bit, so hang tight. For now, just **come up with a list of five to ten exercises for each body part with whatever apparatus(s) you may have, even if it is just your own body weight.** You may choose to go to the gym, or have a few dumbbells, resistance bands and a stability ball laying around in the house. Use whatever you have available to you.

You must understand, though, that burning fat is much more likely to happen with resistance training than without: And fat is what you want to get rid of, not weight. Losing fat off your body will make you lose inches, but not necessarily weight. With losing fat you will look like you've lost fifteen or twenty pounds, but actually may not have lost any, and that is perfectly fine.

CHAPTER 24

WE ALL NEED SOME SORT OF CARDIOVASCULAR TRAINING

EVEN THOUGH WE BURN MORE FAT WITH RESISTANCE TRAINING, IT is still very important to get some cardiovascular training in as well. Cardio is good for many reasons when done correctly. First, cardio training makes the heart and lungs stronger. After all, they are muscles too. And, as I said before, cardiovascular training does burn some fat (to a certain point. Plus doing cardio makes us feel better and improves our mood.

Cardiovascular training can be done in many different forms: Walking, running, biking, swimming can all be done outside. I personally love doing cardio outside whenever possible as being outside in nature, in the elements is much better for the mind. **Try doing an outdoor activity at least once per week to rejuvenate and clear the mind.**

There are also many cardiovascular machines that can be used such as a treadmill, elliptical, rowing machine, spin bike, Peloton bike and Peloton treadmill, even fitness boxing. Almost everyone these days has some piece of cardiovascular machine in their homes, like a treadmill or recumbent bike.

Now listen as this is very important. When it comes to cardiovascular training there is a certain point where the body stops pulling from fat for energy and starts pulling from muscle instead. Everyone burns fat at a slightly different pace, but a good rule of thumb to follow for fat burning is no more than forty five minutes for cardiovascular training. It's usually sooner than that but I always use that as a maximum for fat burning before we start burning away muscle instead of fat.

There are many ways to do cardiovascular training. We've all seen or heard of the different heart rate zones. Without knowing your personal zone numbers, an easy way to know if you are in your fat burning zone when doing cardiovascular training is being aware of how you are breathing. If you are able to talk and carry on a conversation, but have to take a deep breath about every sentence or every other sentence, you are most likely in your fat burning zone. If you can talk to someone with no problem, not taking any deep breaths you are most likely not in the fat burning zone yet and you'll need to push just a bit harder. On the other end, if you have a lot of heavy breathing and find it hard to talk, you are probably above your fat burning zone and need to ease off a little.

Now here's the kicker! I'm sure you've all heard of HIIT training. The means High Intense Interval Training. HIIT training is when you combine different heart rate zones and muscle groups within the same workout. Moving from slower, controlled exercises to high intensity movements. An example of this with cardiovascular exercise would be moving from a power-walk for one or two minutes, breathing easy, to thirty seconds or one minute of sprinting as hard as possible so you become completely out of breath. Then dropping back down again, over and over for about thirty minutes. This is also a form of interval training. This type of training burns much more fat than just staying in your comfortable fat burning zone. I personally love HIIT or interval training for most of my cardiovascular and strength workouts, but do recommend one cardio workout per week staying in your fat burning zone. Changing up the types of training is good to do, but I also like to be as efficient as possible when it comes to fat burning. Plus when life is so hectic and everyone has no time to workout because their lives are so chaotic, HIIT training makes a lot of sense. Getting more done in less time is something we all need. People think they have to work out for hours upon hours to have any success. That simply isn't the case. Any time you have to get in a good HIIT or interval type training session, do it! It just makes a lot of sense. However, please know that there is not one perfect way to burn fat.

As far as how many times per week is needed for cardiovascular training, two to three times each week is great for fat burning. **Again, just thirty to forty minutes of a slow/fast interval workout burns a lot more fat than just doing a moderate pace cardio in your fat burning zone for one hour. Be efficient! Try this.**

CHAPTER 25

BACK TO MOBILITY TRAINING

NOW, LET'S JUMP BACK TO MOBILITY TRAINING. I SKIPPED THIS before because I wanted to come back to this to tell you how important this is as we get older. Taking care of your joints and joint range of motion is so important the older we get. I'm sure you are thinking in our sixties, seventies and beyond. While you are correct, I'm really talking about forty and up.

I always thought I was invincible. Really. I believed I could do anything if I just put my mind to it. I still believe that...to an extent. Now that I'm almost fifty years old as I write this, which is truly hard to believe, it's more of... I can do anything, as long as my joint strength and range of motion is at its best. I have focused so much on my fitness level in the past few years, meaning strength and cardiovascular fitness, I have found that I have forgotten the most important part, which is mobility training. If I don't have mobility, my strength training suffers immensely and my cardiovascular training suffers immensely, which means I'm most likely in pain somewhere in my body, and my overall fitness level is not nearly what it could be.

Honestly, it's the pain part that I want to get rid of. I hate to be in pain, and I hate it even more when I see others in pain. **By working** on mobility training just one or even two days per week I promise you will be in much less pain. And as we all get older, which we all do, that is something we all try to avoid.

I have added a lot of mobility back into my everyday routine and now is a very big part of my training programs at CannonFit. Now that I'm older and have lived and learned I'm better for it and I'm helping more and more people be better because of it. You should do the same.

CHAPTER 26

COMBINING THEM ALL TOGETHER

NOW THAT YOU KNOW WE ALL NEED STRENGTH TRAINING, CARdiovascular training, and some mobility, combining them is definitely something to think about. It's easy to combine the first two. However, sometimes when you do this, it's good to add another ten to fifteen minutes to your overall workout, but not always.

If you have time to do a good forty five minute full-go workout like I give in my CannonFit training studio try something like this;

Do one or two upper body exercises, again with whatever equipment you have available to you if any, then add a quick one minute of high intensity cardio such as running up and down the stairs or doing jumping jacks or a fast run on a treadmill. Do two or three sets of this with no rest, then do the same type of thing with lower body exercises.

This, for the most part, keeps the heart rate up in the fat burning zone for most of the workout, but also gets the heart rate just above the fat burning zone (the anaerobic zone). By moving from the lower part of the fat burning zone to the high end of the anaerobic zone over and over again, more fat will be burned in a short amount of time. This is exactly what we want when trying to lose fat.

There are many different types of formats or "programming" I recommend that makes life a bit easier and are very effective. Let's get into those in the next chapter.

They key in combining the strength and cardiovascular exercises together is to move the heart rate from a lower heart rate to a higher heart rate over and over. This can be done in short, faster segments or long, slower segments. The strength training could be done for five to ten minutes with a few exercises, then five to ten minutes of higher intensity cardio. These would be longer segments. Or a shorter time of strength such as two minutes of two strength exercises, moving straight into a fast one minute greater intense cardio. This is a shorter, faster type segment. Both work very well. And both should be done. Mixing up the programming is a great thing to do so the body doesn't get used to doing the same thing over and over again. If that happens the body might go into a plateau, until you switch things up. Of course, a few good mobility type warm up exercises or even cool down movements are great to begin or finish off the workout.

Try coming up with a few workouts like this and see how you like it. Also see how much you will get done in such a short amount of time. No more walking into a gym and talking in front of machines for hours!

CHAPTER 27

YOU DON'T ALWAYS HAVE TO JOIN A GYM

ONCE A DECISION IS FINALLY MADE TO MAKE A CHANGE FOR THE body so many people run straight to the gym and get a long membership that really isn't needed. The major thing that *is* needed however, something we all need for success, is *accountability*. Joining a gym isn't necessarily the best accountability as there is no set schedule, no standing appointments, no one waiting for you, and no lost payment for missing. The monthly gym membership is usually a minimal cost to most people, so if you miss a few days, or a month, or two it's really not a big deal to you.

You don't need that. Gyms are great for those that don't need accountability, don't get me wrong. But everyone needs accountability to get results and big membership style gyms just don't offer that. All those fancy machines and nice looking equipment are great, but fancy and nice looking don't hold you accountable for showing up. Neither does the free towel service or a nice locker room to change in.

Look, if you want results, go back and read chapter 15 again. It's all about accountability. Do everything I said in that chapter and get it done at home. It's easy to set a workout time in your own daily calendar. Use it, set the alarm for it. Plan on it. If it's on your daily calendar you are more likely to do it. If you have a few dumbbells and bands, that's really all you need. During the COVID forty-five day lockdown here in South Carolina, I got into the best shape I've been in years, all from home. I used four different sets of dumbbells, one resistance band I tied to our basketball hoop outside, our swing set, an old agility ladder which I could have drawn out with my youngest son's outdoor chalk, a BOSU ball, and a yoga mat. I did my cardio walking and jogging through the neighborhood and town. Never once did I use the elliptical or spin bike I have in my house. I always did my strength workouts outside on our patio or in the garage if it rained. I worked out at 9am everyday no matter what. It was in my daily calendar. Guess what? Every one of my clients did their workouts at home during that lockdown as well. I sent them workouts with exercises from my YouTube channel. For forty-five days, they all did it. You can too!

It's easy to find home equipment for not much money. It's another story to come up with the correct routines according to your goals. Let me help you with this. Below are a few formats I use on a daily basis in my own personal training studio. You can use these to get a great workout routine going right away.

Keep in mind as you read through these that the repetitions can be changed to your liking, or change per workout, so one workout may be twenty repetitions and the next time you do that same workout it could be heavier weights but only ten repetitions. You can even change the repetitions to timed exercises. So, instead of reps, try doing each exercise for forty-five seconds with fifteen seconds to get to the next exercise. It's completely up to you so play around with it: have fun with it. Make the workouts your own, but challenge yourself.

ROUTINE 1:

- Back exercise 10-20 reps
- Leg exercise (quads) 10-20 reps -Core exercise 10-20 reps Repeat 2-3 sets with no rest
- Cardio 3-4 minutes chest exercise 10-20 reps -leg exercise (hamstring) core exercise 10-20 reps Repeat 2-3 sets with no rest
- Cardio 3-4 minutes shoulder exercise 10-20 reps -leg exercise (gluteals) 10-20 reps core exercise 10-20 reps
- Repeat 2-3 sets with no rest
- Cardio 3-4 mintes

ROUTINE 2:

- Back exercise timed
- Biceps exercise timed
- Core exercise timed
- HIIT cardio (such as jumping jax or burpees) timed
- Repeat 3-4 sets with no rest chest exercise timed -triceps exercise timed core exercise timed
- HIIT cardio timed
- Repeat 3-4 sets with no rest leg with shoulder exercise timed leg with shoulder exercise timed -core exercise timed
- HIIT cardio timed
- Repeat 3-4 sets with no rest

ROUTINE 3:

- Shoulder exercise 15 reps triceps exercise 15 reps

- Biceps exercise 15 reps
- Repeat 2-3 sets
- 2 minute harder jog/run -leg (quad) 15 reps leg (hamstring) 15 reps leg (gluteals) 15 reps
- Repeat 2-3 sets
- 2 minute running up and down the stairs core exercise 15 reps core exercise 15 reps core exercise 15 reps
- Repeat 2-3 sets

Again, these are just examples of routines you might want to try. There is an unlimited amount of routines that you could come up with. Just have fun with it, enjoy them, and make sure it fits in with your purpose. If you work out without a purpose, what are you working out for?

CHAPTER 28

WE ALL NEED A DAY OF RELAXING ACTIVE RECOVERY

I OFTEN WONDER HOW MANY PEOPLE MAKE RECOVERY AND RELAX-ation a priority. My bet is not too many. However, most people that read this book are likely over the age of twenty-five, and certain parts of the body, such as the brain, actually start breaking down much earlier in our lives than we think. Then things like the muscles start going in the early thirties and a whole lot of things start to deteriorate once we hit forty.

You can see how important it is to take care of your body once you get older. I was one of those people that said I wouldn't start deteriorating until much later than everyone else because of my lifestyle. I have lived healthy all my life, ate well, and have always worked out. I have never drank or smoked. Well, I was certainly wrong about that. It may have hit me later, but when one thing started to break down a lot of things soon followed. Even though I was a long jumper and sprinter for fifteen plus years, I never had knee problems. Then in what seemed like an instant, they both started really hurting. I mean hurting bad! I pushed through, though, because I have that male ego going on, the one that says "You still got it Chad." Then the stay at home quarantine hit because of COVID and I was running like a fiend, strength training more and harder than ever before, and playing basketball with my son almost every night. Then on May 17th, 2020 I tore my meniscus playing basketball with my son. He says he broke my ankles, because that sounds cool, but my knees were already hurting and I didn't slow down to ever let my body fully or even partially recover. I guess my right knee decided that it had enough. I battled that injury for months with therapy, and finally succumbed to surgery. It's now been six months since that surgery and I'm having another surgery on the same knee in about a week and a half from the time I am writing this book because my body has decided to grow a lot of scar tissue, some of which had jammed up under my kneecap.

Before all this happened, I never took the time to recover. I'm talking recovery of the muscles, the joints, the bones, and even the brain. I thought I was better than that. I was also being an idiot. Now I know better. It's not that I didn't know about it, I just didn't really practice it. I made my clients do things to recover, but personally I didn't do any of it nearly enough, probably because I didn't think I was at the point yet. It's dumb to think of waiting to do things for recovery before you actually need it. I've learned the hard way that if you start intentionally recovering and relaxing your body, you will have a much less injury prone lifestyle.

Now I stretch, use a muscle stimulation unit (PowerDot), get massages, use a hand held massage gun (PureWave), eat more for recovery, cool down more after workouts, use muscle rubs and creams, use oils, get the proper amount of sleep, and most of all I take relaxing and recovering my brain very, very seriously. It's an amazing feeling once you let your mind recover from all the things it goes through and thinks about each and every day.

I'm going to go over about a dozen things in the coming chapters that all have to do with recovery for the body and mind, and relaxation to help the body and mind to be rejuvenated and ready for what's next. Even if you never have any kind of transformation or never achieve any weight loss, but work hard on the different things I'm about to share with you, I guarantee you will live a much healthier, pain free, less stressful life. For most people, that's a life worth living.

CHAPTER 29

SLEEP

FOR SOME REASON FROM THE TIME I WAS AN OLDER TEENAGER IN high school, all through college and up until now I have always taken sleep very seriously. I have always known how important it is for me to be at my best the next day through good sleep. I never really knew why it helped until the last five or ten years, but just knew it did. Now that I know about sleep patterns, dreaming behaviors, what the appropriate time of sleep we need for the goals we have, what sleep does to the metabolism, mind, and joint recovery, I understand how important and how serious we should take our sleeping behaviors. This is something that should not be taken for granted, ever. **If you really want to achieve the highest results you can (in anything you do) you need to make sleep a top priority in your life.** I truly believe this.

Since I was a senior in high school, I have had an unwritten bedtime that I have tried to be very faithful to: 10:00PM. That's my time. In high school, I knew that if I went to bed around 10:00PM I would get enough rest and be refreshed the next day to kick some major tail as an elite level track athlete. I wish now that I knew it was better for academics as well, but that wasn't my focus then, at all!

I did this all through college as well. I was a serious athlete in college and didn't mess around because if I didn't have my track career in college I wasn't going to be in college and who knows where I would be today if that were the case? So, yes, even as a college student, when everyone else was out partying and drinking, my butt went to bed by 10:00PM most nights. I had goals and very big dreams and knew that my sleep was crucial.

The advice I have for you on sleep is simply this; The body is at its best the next day when it has enough REM sleep or "good" sleep as I call it. Usually when you are dreaming, you are in a good REM sleep. This happens when the body gets about seven—eight hours of sleep a night on average for adults, eight—nine hours for young adults, and nine to ten hours for young teenagers.

Back when I started my business, I learned that the people who work harder work more hours. The ones who only sleep three—four hours every night early in their career are the ones that become successful. Now that I'm an older and wiser business owner, I say that advice I learned was a bunch of cow doo doo! You can only work as hard as your body lets you. You can try to push through, and you can push through up until a point, then your body breaks. Remember the chapter on consistency. Consistency is the key to rewards: not trying hard or going all out then dying from mental and physical fatigue.

Personally, I try to get seven hours of sleep every night. I get up to start my day by 5:00AM on the weekdays. So all I do is count the hours backwards seven hours, which puts me at a 10:00PM bedtime. That doesn't mean get in bed by 10:00, that means already in bed, no TV, no book, no phone, no social media. Lights out by 10:00PM. On the weekends, I always try to get eight hours of sleep, but my body just has its own clock I guess and most of the time my body just automatically wakes up at 5:00AM. So **whatever time you need to be up by in the mornings, just count back seven hours and that is your** bed-time.

If you are a night owl and like to stay up late, get a few late shows in, eat a few snacks, and relax your brain until midnight or later, I have news for you, you aren't relaxing at all! Most likely, you are actually mentally and physically running your body down even more. And by the end of the day, or when you get home from work and running the kids around you are just so exhausted you most likely just want to collapse. But you don't, instead you stay up late again and again, night after night because that's your routine. You might think it's relaxing, but it's actually hurting you even more.

Your brain must relax. Most people turn on the TV late at night or scroll through social media, including myself. However, if the tendency to do this is less than seven hours before you have to get up, you aren't doing yourself any favors. Watching a show on TV ignites the brain even more. You might not be thinking about work but on a different scale your brain is working in overdrive trying to figure out who committed the crime on that particular show, or how to improve your house, or who's going to win the bake off. If you must have the TV on, try watching something that isn't attention grabbing like a football game with two teams you aren't really interested in: Something that you could turn off without waiting to see what happens in the end.

The goal is to let your body and mind relax, not hype it up again. I try to limit my TV time at night. Instead I'll fill my brain with educational things like a good motivating, inspirational or educational book, an audio book where I can just close my eyes and listen. All through college and until I got married, I always listened to relaxing, meditating music with no words. I loved that. I even had a few cassettes (Yes, I said cassettes) of ocean sounds or forest sounds. There are apps like that now. Probably the best-known app is called Calm.

Over my thirty plus years of being a fitness coach I've seen one thing that almost never changes; Those that stay up late end up gaining weight. That is one constant I've seen over my professional career. On the opposite end, I've also seen those that get up before the sun have been the healthiest, fittest people. There are many studies on this out there and I hear it all the time from all my coaching groups, masterminds, and mentors. They all say that the healthiest, fittest and most successful people are the ones that get up before sunrise. It's absolutely true!

Once you get good sleep, there are a few keys to waking up that are very critical for you having a better day. Fist I learned a few years ago that the most successful businesspeople in the world wake up before their alarm goes off before 5:00AM. Notice I said before their alarm goes off. They just wake up. Do you have any idea why that happens? I'll tell you... Because these people are looking forward to conquering their day. They can't wait to get up and attack the day. Are you one of those people? Or do you hate getting up, hate going to work, would rather stay in bed and sleep the day away? If your answer is the ladder you have a serious problem about what career you are in. If you don't automatically wake up most days before your alarm goes off and would rather sleep than go to work or get whatever kind of day you have started, you need to consider a new career in my opinion, one that you look forward to. I would say that six out of seven days I wake up around 4:55AM—before my alarm goes off. Yes, I'm groggy and I'm moving slowly because it is the morning, but my mind is excited to get working on what I want to get working on. I'm excited to go see my clients. I'm excited to be a 6:00AM motivator. I'm excited to get up at 4:50AM this Saturday morning to work on this book.

A pet peeve of mine is hitting the snooze button on the alarm. Oh man, that really aggravates me. My wife does it...Twice. I don't hold it against her though. There is usually one day each week that I start training clients a little later, so I'll hear her alarm go off. She wakes up to hit snooze, and nine minutes later, she does it again. Nine minutes later she finally gets up. In the last year I'll say she has done a better job of doing it just once. But still, to me it really makes zero sense as to why anyone would think hitting the snooze button helps in any way. People say that it helps them slowly wake up. I don't understand that either. To me that just makes me groggy. To me, you just lost some valuable sleep time. So as soon as you wake up or when that alarm goes off, just sit right up, do a few stretches and off you go. I promise you will feel better.

CHAPTER 30

SUPPLEMENTS

THIS IS A SUBJECT THAT I COULD ALSO MAKE INTO AN ENTIRE BOOK. I'm going to be as straight forward and honest as I can here; **If you have any kind of weight loss, fat loss, fitness, sport, or health related goal you 100% need to be taking supplementation.**

Eating the food we eat in today's world just isn't what it used to be. With the foods we have access to and eat on a regular basis I believe that we just don't get the vitamins, minerals and nutrients that the body truly needs to sustain a healthy, energetic life, not to mention being able to perform in the life that you want.

We should all be taking some sort of multivitamin for overall wellness. This is a must in my opinion. A lot of people say that if we eat the food we should then taking a multivitamin isn't necessary. So, let me ask you this: How many people do you know eat the foods they should eat on a day-to-day basis and nothing else? No-one I know, including all my clients, athletes, friends and family, even myself don't eat what our bodies completely need. We simply don't get all the foods needed to get us to our optimum health and performance on a daily basis. We don't: Honestly no-one does. I don't know you, but I'm guessing that you don't either. So, if you don't take a multivitamin, why not? What's it going to hurt?

As we get older I believe that we all need to take more protein and joint help as well. The body starts breaking down in our thirties for the most part. **We all need to increase our protein intake to keep more muscle and burn more fat.** Supplements are a great solution for that. **We also need to keep our joints working as normally as possible for the longest we can.** Supplements to help joint health are a great way to stay feeling good, especially if you beat up your joints as I did when I was younger. There are other supplements that I recommend you also take like Omega's. These can help with everything from cholesterol to metabolism to skin and eye health.

Now let's talk a bit about athletes and supplements. How many professional athletes do you see taking some type of supplementation? My guess is a lot. These athletes are trying to get their bodies to perform at high levels and recover better and faster. The everyday Joe does the same thing, just not on a professional athlete level. Your body and my body also work hard to perform at high levels and recover well, so there is no reason why the everyday Joe shouldn't do or take what the everyday pro does.

I completely believe that everyone should take a pre-workout drink to help get more out of their workouts, a post-workout shake to help muscles recover after working them hard, and extra protein to help keep muscle on the body, since it breaks down the older we get.

These are the bare minimum when it comes to supplementation. If you want to personally find out more about what I personally take, or need help figuring out what to take yourself feel free to contact me through social media or my website www.cannonfit.com. I'll be glad to help you.

CHAPTER 31

AROMATHERAPY

I AM A FIRM BELIEVER THAT HOW YOU FEEL IS HOW YOU ACT. IN OTHER words, if you feel energized you act energized. If you feel tired you act tired. There are things available to us that help with the way we feel, like aromatherapy.

If you've never used oils before, you must give it a try. In the late 1990's I had lots of scented candles around my apartments. I did this simply because it smelled good which made me feel good. I think I started that because I dated a girl who had a lot of scented candles in her place and I liked them enough to start getting some myself. Now I wonder sometimes how well it really works because that girl turned out to be a little psycho and that relationship didn't last long. Either way I kept putting scented candles around my apartment.

Oils are a bit different but act in the same way and it has been found that different scents help with different areas of the body. Lemon oil can help clear nasal passages and allow for better breathing. Chamomile helps relieve cold and flu like symptoms. If you have a fever or a virus try using eucalyptus. If you have trouble sleeping try using lavender oils as it helps relieve stress, fatigue, depression and headaches and just helps the brain relax. If you need to feel more energized try using peppermint, rosemary or lemon. There are many different scents that really do help with so many things. My wife has oil diffusers all over our house and is very diligent about having them going. She even brings one to hotels whenever we stay in one as hotel rooms are sometimes musty.

Try using oils around your house, at work or wherever you spend a lot of time and put the correct scents in for how you want to feel.

CHAPTER 32

MASSAGE & ROLLING

THIS IS ONE THING I LOVE TO DO FOR MY BODY. SOMETIMES IT'S A little painful, but well worth a few seconds of being uncomfortable over being in pain all the time.

I have to say that I have one of the best massage therapists ever working out of the CannonFit studio. Abby Rhoades knows her stuff. In fact, I recently had Abby as a guest on my Push-ups & Pizza podcast. She spoke about different types of massages and what each does. My favorite kind is what I call body work, or deep tissue massage. This is something that I have grown to love and understand how important it is especially as we get older and how important it is for athletes.

Below are a few reasons why massage is so important. While I go through these I want you to think if any of these would be helpful to you.

1. Increases muscle and joint range of motion.
2. Decreases pain.
3. Eliminates toxins from the body.
4. Removes unwanted knots.
5. Improves energy.
6. Increases weight loss.

Would any of those things be something you might need?

What about things like helping with sciatic issues, migraine relief, relief of plantar fasciitis, occipital release, I.T. Band release, improvement of your golf or tennis game, being able to play with your kids, or sleep better? These are usual things that people want to improve. Body work or deep tissue massage does wonders for the body and you can't possibly get enough of it, especially if you're one that works out on a regular basis.

Try getting a deep tissue massage once or even twice each month to help your body recover and repair. Most people will get a massage after something happens like an injury and if they are in pain, but if you start getting deep tissue massages for prevention regularly it will change your whole world.

A few other things I highly recommend are foam rolling and using a handheld roller. Rolling out your muscles helps release any lactic acid build up and any knots that might have formed that have already caused stress or pain. I was at one of my physical therapy appointments not long ago for my recovering knee surgery and Scott Kathmann, my therapist from Elite Physical Therapy, rolled out my I.T. Band before I did a few strength exercises to release some of the built up knots that formed from being dormant for a few months. I was not happy with him because it was painful! Honestly I wanted to punch him in the nose, but I didn't because I knew I needed it. From not using my leg for a few months before my surgery and then after the surgery most of my leg had atrophied and knotted up. If you haven't worked out, been sedentary or have not put your muscles and joints through full range of motion in a while, your muscles need to be rolled out! If you work out regularly and put your muscles in stress mode, you need to help your muscles recover with some rolling.

Another device I use quite a bit is something I got a few years ago called a PureWave. It's a handheld massage gun. There are many different devices like this that people love. I personally use the

PureWave almost daily for a few minutes on the spots where I'm most tense or have knots. Abby, my massage therapist recommends using this as much as possible between my sessions with her. My wife loves the PureWave also as she uses it more than I do.

I understand that getting massages can be costly. It's better to spend the money on regular massages though, rather than on the drugs and surgeries you'll need because not taking care of your muscles like I unfortunately did. I am now a regular at getting massages after learning my lesson on waiting until I needed it.

However, a foam roller or a handheld roller are very affordable, costing around $15-$30, and a hand held massage gun can be anywhere from $100 to $500, but last forever and in my opinion should be in everyone's household.

CHAPTER 33

STRETCHING

W E ALL KNOW THAT WE SHOULD BE STRETCHING, BUT FOR MOST of us we never take the time to sit down, relax for ten to fifteen minutes to stretch those muscles. Why do we do this, even though we all know how important it is for our bodies? I think it's because it feels like it takes too much time, and in everyone's hectic lifestyle who has time for that? I also think most people believe that stretching is a painful thing.

Here's the honest truth: We all need to take time to stretch and here's why;

First and foremost, it's relaxing. We don't want to take our stretching to a painful state. It should be a small stretch held for longer periods of time, not stretching our muscles so far that it hurts, thus wanting to stop. Stretching should almost be a meditative type of activity where the focus is on breath. Stretching should relax the mind and rejuvenate the body.

Secondly, stretching keeps the muscles and joints in full range of motion. This is so important when it comes to living a pain free lifestyle. Not keeping the muscles flexible will keep them short and tight which causes other short, tight muscles. This just means body pain, usually in many different places throughout the body. I'm pretty sure that living a pain free life is something everyone wants.

Even though we could have great benefits from stretching daily, I suggest taking at least one or even two days per week and scheduling out thirty minutes for stretching the major muscle groups. Keep it simple: Get a stretching strap and lay down holding a hamstring stretch for two to three minutes for each leg. Then bring the leg out to the side stretching the inner thigh/groin muscles, then bring the leg across the other leg to stretch the I.T. Band. Hold each stretch for two to three minutes. Don't forget the calves. Then some upper body stretches should also be done for the chest, back and shoulders. If you don't know what to do just go to YouTube and type in chest stretches or back stretches, or anything you want to stretch.

Stretching is one of the most important parts of taking care of your body. If I were to pick one thing I could always do now, it would be stretching. Stretching would be over strength training and cardiovascular training. I would say it's almost even with proper nutrition. That's how important stretching is.

Take the time to stretch. Schedule it into your day and make it a habit. This is probably one of the best pieces of advice I'm giving out of the entire book, so please take stretching seriously.

CHAPTER 34

HEAT, ICE & CRYOTHERAPY

THE QUESTION I HAVE BEEN ASKED MOST OFTEN OVER THE PAST thirty years is "Should I use heat or ice?" This is tricky for most people. Here's the rule of thumb to follow when it comes to heat and ice:

Use ice for acute injuries ,or pain, or when there is swelling and inflammation. A good ice pack wrapped in a pillowcase can be put directly on the injury for about ten minutes. Use heat when there is muscle soreness. Moist heat, like a steamed towel, may be slightly more effective than dry heat such as a heating pad, but both are good. Make sure, though, that it's just warm, not hot.

As a college athlete I was told by our athletic trainer to do hot-cold therapy every day for prevention, as well as to use for any injuries I may already had. This meant I went from five minutes of an ice bath (yes, this means a tub of water with many large buckets of ice poured into it) up to my chest then moving to five minutes in a hot tub, usually a three-cycle sequence. I will never forget doing this for four straight years. I usually did this twice per day. Honestly it was probably one of the best things I've ever done for my body. What this does is bring a lot of good blood cells to any injury that may be there or starting to flair up to help recovery happen much faster. Honestly, I hated the first year of this, but after that I remember that I actually started looking forward to those times as it made my body feel so much better.

So it is still a good idea to add hot-cold therapy to any injury or muscle aches. Simply use a hot, moist compress for five minutes, then switch to an ice pack for five minutes. If you want an even better effect keep moving back and forth between the two a few times.

Most of us have now heard about Cryotherapy. This is a trend that has become increasingly popular. With Cryotherapy a person sits or stands in a very cold dry ice tank for three to five minutes. Pain relief and muscle healing are the main reasons people are flocking to Cryotherapy. Although it is fairly new and not a lot of studies are out on Cryotherapy, it does make a lot of sense to me. I've even thought about putting them into my training studio, but have not pulled the trigger because the cost of just one Cryo tube is too much for my budget right now. It would be great to have one though. **I would use Cryotherapy all the time. Most places charge $35-$75 for each session, so for injury prevention or helping an injury recover more quickly I believe it's worth the money.**

CHAPTER 35

RED-LIGHT THERAPY

RED LIGHT THERAPY IS CATCHING ON QUICKLY ALL OVER THE world. This type of therapy uses low-level wavelengths of red or near inferred light mainly to treat skin issues such as scars, wounds, and wrinkles. Red light therapy not only heals skin issues but also muscle tissue and other things such as dementia, dental pain, hair loss, osteoarthritis, and tendinitis.

Most would say that I should use it for my hair loss because I am as bald as they come, but actually I personally need Red light therapy for osteoarthritis and tendonitis in my joints, mainly my knees.

Let's say that you just had a hard strength training workout and your muscles are darn sore. Red light therapy would be great to help the muscle tissue recover much quicker than normal. More and more people these days are using red light therapy for these reasons: mainly athletes. This is simply because they know more about it. But it's great for everyone. I know that many chiropractors, massage therapists and other health service-related businesses in my area are starting to offer red light therapy as part of their services so it's definitely catching on.

Anyone can buy a small or large red light therapy bed (or strip of lights) on the web. One of the most popular is PlatinumLED

Therapy Lights. I've considered putting this in my own studio for clients to use after their training sessions also. I do believe it's worth it, especially after hardcore workouts or for an injury.

CHAPTER 36

RECOVERY BEDDING, SLEEPWEAR & EYE MASKS

THIS IS A COOL TOPIC IN MY OPINION. LET'S START WITH RECOVery bedding and sleepwear. I know there are a few different versions available on the market, but I'll mention one that most people might know. Under Armour has their own version of both sheets and sleepwear as well as an entire Recover (TM) apparel line that a few of my trainer friends use and recommend. They all love them! There are also many other brands available. The technology is made to put energy back into the body, which helps recovery happen quicker. Many people use them both as both have caught on quickly around the world. **Start using recovery bedding and recovery sleepwear.**

Let me talk about eye masks now. About eight months ago I started sleeping with an eye mask. Before I started using this my sleeping habits were horrendous to say the least. Some nights I slept okay, some I didn't sleep at all, others I tossed and turned and was in and out of sleep. I never really had a good night sleep. For me I blame it on my own brain. My brain is continuously going, thinking, dreaming of things I have to do, haven't done yet, or dream of doing. My brain just never stops. If I turn over in the middle of the night I start thinking. If I hear a noise and wake up for a split-second my brain starts to think and once it starts I have trouble turning it off.

After I started using an eye mask, my sleeping habits instantly changed and have been really good for the entire eight months that I've been using it. I didn't get anything special. I just got something for men from the grocery store that I happened to see one day.

At first my kids and even my wife made fun of me because I looked funny, but I honestly didn't care at that point. My sleeping patterns were so bad and it seemed like I was tired all the time so no matter what I looked like or who made fun of me I was going to try it. Right away it worked. I stopped thinking all the time. Little things didn't wake me up anymore. It was honestly a game changer in my world.

Since I didn't get the best mask, I had to make some adjustments to it. There is a velcro strap that attached the two ends together in the back and since I'm completely bald the velcro rubs against the skin on my head which left a nice mark the first night, so I put something over it and that seemed to work. The mask also falls off at least once each night, so I have to find it in the dark and put it back on. I have asked a few other friends of mine, mostly other trainers if they recommend a certain mask and they all said the Sleep Master Sleep Mask is the one to get. So, of course, I ordered one. It's amazingly comfortable and was very affordable. I absolutely love it and I'm so glad I switched to it. The only downfall to it is that my wife pointed out to me that the fabric I got is a blueish color, and our sheets are white. After a few weeks a nice blue stain has shown up on the white pillowcase. It probably needs to be washed before using it, but to this point I haven't looked up how it needs to be washed. Shame on me. I guess it's time for new (colorful) sheets, because I'm never giving up my Sleep Master Sleep Mask. It has changed my life forever!

If you are one that has trouble sleeping, please try a sleep mask. I truly believe in them. I have stopped thinking so much all night long, I fall asleep much faster, and stay asleep longer.

CHAPTER 37

COMPRESSION SLEEVES AND SOCKS

O VER THE PAST FIFTEEN YEARS OR SO COMPRESSION SLEEVES HAVE grown popular. Look, we all have aches and pains especially in our limbs and we could use the help any way we can get it to be in less pain. These days you see almost everyone wear compression sleeves on all levels of track & field and cross country teams, people running 5K road races, half marathons and full marathons. Everyone seems to wear lower leg compression sleeves. You also see professional basketball players wear them on their legs and arms. In fact, there are people in every type of sport now that use some type of compression sleeve somewhere on their body. They are just that popular. I started wearing compression socks in 2011 when I ran the Savannah Rock'n Roll Marathon. I truly believe they helped me immensely!

What compression sleeves do is bring oxygen rich blood to the muscles. This blood is filled with nutrients and hydration which helps flush out lactic acid and improve circulation to that particular body part while helping the healing process. Compression socks and leg sleeves can also reduce vibration, which can improve muscle efficiency and mechanics which is why I first used them. I needed all the help I could get in my first marathon as I really didn't know what I was getting myself into.

Now, after my two knee surgeries I use a compression leg sleeve over my knee. I use this while I work because I'm on my feet for hours demonstrating different movements. This helps me feel like my leg has more stability, is functioning correctly and not having any parts moving in and out of proper alignment.

There are so many people that use compression sleeves on arms, legs, even shoulders and swear by them. Others don't like them. Me personally, I like them a lot and feel a huge benefit from them. **My suggestion is that compression is definitely worth a try. Don't try it once either. There are so many different brands, maybe you had one brand that might not have felt good to you and you need to try a different brand.** The science is there and I trust the science behind them. But again, it's personal preference if you want to use them or not.

CHAPTER 38

SHOES AND SHOE INSERTS

IF YOU DON'T HAVE THE CORRECT SHOES ON YOUR FEET THAT YOUR body properly needs, you just don't know how much better you could feel! It is an amazing idea to see what type of foot you have, which then tells you what type of shoe you should have on your feet.

There are running stores or shoe stores all around the world that give free foot testing to see what type of shoe fits your feet the best. You might have low arches, high arches, neutral arches. You might pronate or supinate. Everyone should know what their feet do. If you have the wrong type of shoes on your feet you could be causing further injury to your feet, knees, hips, or even low back. Getting your feet tested is something I recommend to all my clients. Basically, you stand on something that takes an imprint and tells you what your feet are doing, or what type of feet you have. After doing this you'll then know what type of shoe your feet need. It is that simple. I had a bad case of plantar fasciitis for almost three years, and after I tried guessing at my shoes, seeing a doctor, getting cortisone shots and trying expensive orthotics I finally decided to get my feet tested, which was absolutely free. I found out that I didn't have much of an arch and that I needed a neutral or stability type shoe, which most athletic type shoes are now labeled as such, and the very nice guy that worked at the store where I had my feet tested, The Palmetto Running Company in Bluffton, South Carolina, suggested that I also try some inserts to go into those shoes that are very specific to my low arches, which I did. I still wear those inserts three years later. I also asked the nice guy about slides that I can wear around the house instead of shoes. I ended up getting some great slides that helped with low arches. I still use and love my slides! In fact, I'm not sure what I would do without them. Within three months of having the proper footwear underneath my body, my feet came alive again, meaning all pain was gone and has been ever since. **Having my feet tested saved me. It was one of the best decisions I have ever made and recommend everyone do so! Go get your feet tested!**

CHAPTER 39

KEEPING TRACK!

W HAT I'M ABOUT TO GO OVER IS A BIG STEP TO ANY KIND OF success you plan on having. Once you know what you want, know why you want it, find as much accountability as possible, add tons of self-motivation, always keep educating yourself, start some sort of exercise program, eat to be healthy and fit, then get a plan of attack and be as consistent as possible. As I said before consistency is everything. Remember the 80/20 rule. Be consistent 80% of the time and be okay with getting off track the other 20%. Just be okay with that. It won't kill your goals. It will only make them and you stronger. Also, the BIG one; know that there WILL always be obstacles that find you. Goals are never met with a straight line. There will always be ups and downs, backward, forward and zig zagged lines. Plan for those obstacles. Be ready to break through, jump over or go around those walls. It might take some time but eventually it will happen if you keep pushing.

I want you to think about starting off, if you haven't already, by doing this one thing each week. **Every Sunday write down the top three WINS that you had over the last seven days.** This could be anything from business, something personal, something with the kids or spouse or the whole family. This could also be specifically associated towards your goal. Something like I was able to get in breakfast every day this week, or I got at least seven hours of sleep on Monday through Friday, or I burned 350 calories through some sort of exercise every day this week.

Hopefully you'll have a lot more wins than just three. The wins I want you to write down are the best of the best. The absolute top three: The wins that make you really proud of achieving.

Next I want you to write your top three failures you had over the week. What things really made you mad, discouraged, or sad? Those are what you write down. Hopefully there won't be too many failures. Just remember that when you fail you can always get back up, shake it off and try again. We learn by seeing our failures. That's why I want you to write them down. This is a very important step.

Lastly, write your top three goals you want or need to attain during the week coming up to help you reach your overall goal. There will be lots of goals, but just pick the three that will really help propel you towards your end goal. And those are what you focus on accomplishing over the next seven days.

Once you do this, you ABSOLUTELY, WITHOUT A DOUBT, HAVE TO share all this with at least one person. One person that will encourage you, listen to you and keep you accountable without babying you.

Start doing this weekly. Every Sunday take five to ten minutes and get this done. By doing this one little thing I promise it will propel you to a better future. A future you want; A future worth fighting for. Here's the cool thing: If you keep these and look back on them a year from now, or even two or three years from now, you might laugh at how easy some of those goals were when you started out: The same goals you once had difficulty with. A year or two after you start I bet your goals will be at a higher level. A level that you didn't think you could get to at first and you couldn't even imagine going for. These are always great to look back on. You will appreciate your journey a lot more when you see it on paper. So never throw these away. Just make this a weekly journal entry. That will make it a bit easier to keep.

Here is something I picked up just a few weeks ago and I believe I'm going to start doing it. I believe I got it from one of the stories in Tim Ferriss' book called Tools of Titans. Tim said that he started something called a jar of awesome. He got a large jar and put it in his kitchen so he saw it every day to remind him about all the awesomeness he has. He said that every day he writes something awesome that happened that day and placed it in that jar. I thought that was the coolest idea when I heard it. It was so cool that I pulled out my phone and wrote "Jar of Awesome" in my notes so I would remember to do it myself. The idea of writing just one awesome thing that happened each day, no matter how small it was is such a great idea. Even if it was just waking up that morning. After all waking up is always a good thing. It means you're not dead. So maybe this is something we could all do. I know the more positive vibes in my life, the better. I'm sure it's the same for everyone so maybe this is something you may start doing as well.

CHAPTER 40

WALKING THE WIRE

LOVE THE SONG "WALKING THE WIRE" BY IMAGINE DRAGONS. IT says it all for me. Why, you ask? Well, the words in the title of the song say it all. "Walking The Wire". To me it means how you are going to approach your purpose or your goal.

I have a great example of this. Imagine you are on the roof top of the tallest building on earth. Now imagine that your young child is on the roof top of the building next to you that is the same height. That building is just twenty feet away. Now all of the sudden the building that your child is on catches on fire and your child has to get off that building, fast! Now you happen to have a wooden board one foot wide sitting on your rooftop that is long enough to put across the two buildings. Would you walk across that board between the two tallest buildings in the world to get to your child? Then would you take your child back across to the non-burning building?

You know if that same board were on the ground or even a few feet off the ground you would with no doubt go across that board, and probably do it with no problem.

But when you are high up, so high that you can't even see the people on the ground and your child is at risk are you one to "walk the wire" as the song would say? It's all in your perspective. How much do you want it? What are you willing to do to reach your goal? What are you willing to go through for your purpose?

Now is the time to decide that you will either do whatever it takes to reach your goal or you decide that you will only do so much. Are you All-In **or not?**

CHAPTER 41

BE AN INSPIRATION TO OTHERS!

Let me ask you... **What will your legacy be?** Just as I said way back in Chapter 8, I'm asking you to really consider what you want your legacy to be. **If you die tomorrow and your family and friends have to write a saying on your gravestone, what do you think they would write about you?** Is it something you want to be remembered for? Is it something you would be proud of? Is it something that you aren't proud of? Be an inspiration to others, your family, your kids, the people you may lead. Be an inspiration to them by your actions, by the effort you put towards reaching success. The effort you show will rub off on thousands of people throughout your lifetime, good or bad, so make it the best you possibly can. Your successes may cause others to be successful. Your failures may cause others to fail. **If you strive to inspire just one person each day you will make a huge difference in the world. It doesn't matter what you accomplish or not accomplish in life. What matters is how you went about trying to succeed at everything.**

CHAPTER 42

FAITH

AITH—IT ALL COMES DOWN TO THIS. IT REALLY DOES. HAVING trust and faith that you will be able to accomplish whatever you want to accomplish. Having faith in yourself to do what it takes to accomplish your goals. Having faith that you will get through your set-backs and push through towards your goals again. Having faith in the people around you helping you along the way. Having faith in the people that might be coaching you, such as me and what's in this book. Having faith in those that are cheering you on. Having faith and trust in the process. And the BIG one, having faith and trust in the lord above that He will lead you, guide you and have your back during the entire process, in everything you do.

I have a saying on my CannonFit studio wall that says "I can do all things... Phil 4:13". Believe that you can do all things with your faith in yourself and because of Him. If you don't believe in yourself, if you don't believe that He has your back, it's going to be so much harder than you can even imagine. That's not how you want to approach attaining your passion. Approach it with the attitude of having faith within you and behind you. God has your back in whatever you endeavor and you must trust that He is with you, He will guide you and He has a plan for you, even if it's not what you think it is.

Many of you might know of the famous 400 meter hurdler, world record holder, Olympian and woman of high faith, Sydney Mclaughlin. Being a track guy myself, I love watching Sydney compete in the 400 hurdles and honestly in any event she runs in. The reason why is not because she's lightning fast. It's also not because she's the best at what she does, and not by the way she competes against her competitors. The reason I love watching her is because I can see that she is competing only against one person. That person being herself. Sydney has found faith in God and trust that He has her back and whatever happens is for the best, in the way she practices, prepares, competes and everything else she does. She trusts that He has her. She has true faith! **You need to have the same faith in your life, and definitely in the journey you are taking towards your goal.**

FINAL THOUGHT...

I HOPE YOU ENJOYED THIS BOOK AS MUCH AS I HAD FUN WRITING IT. Hopefully you learned a few things along the way and will put the information you did learn into action. That's the main thing...**take action.** Once you take action I know you will get results and find your Wooooo!

I'm going to end this book with a wise piece of information that one of my favorite clients, Mona Huff, once told me. Mona told me that she uses three mantras for her entire life. I loved them so much and believe in them myself I just had to share them with you...

1.   Family FIRST
2.   If you can't laugh it AIN'T worth it
3.   The most important things in life AREN'T things

Think about that! WOOOOO!

ACKNOWLEDGEMENTS

D REAMS ARE WHAT MAKE UP OUR LIVES. WITHOUT THEM CIVILI-
zation wouldn't move forward. Without the help from others
giving us a push to move towards those dreams, from others to give
their knowledge and support to achieve our dreams nothing would
ever happen. Thank you to everyone who has inspired me and has
made me raise my eyebrows with curiosity over my 50 years to help
me always strive to be better.

I want to personally thank a dear friend of mine, Mitch Brown, for
staying on me with my goals, with this book and constantly pushing
and inspiring me to be at least 1% better every day. You're an inspiration and you need to know it.

For my editor Noah Keefer, you are the best! And to my publisher;
Palmetto Publishing, Nicole and Alexandra, I could not have done
this without you.

Thank you, all my clients that stood by me, and dealt with me
during my two knee surgeries and kept inspiring me to push and get
better. I'm supposed to be the one inspiring all of you. But, all of you
help inspire me to overcome.

Speaking of my knee surgeries, I really want to personally thank
a few people that helped get me back during a hard time, all in the
span of a few days.

First, to my neighbors Paulette and Dave. I have cut their grass for
a few years because of their age, health and finances. They saw that I

was having some problems with my knee and the one week I needed it, they paid for someone to mow their own yard and mine, even though I know it was not affordable. There was no way I could have done it that week and somehow you knew. Thank you.

Second, one of my best friends from the state of Ohio, who was vacationing about an hour away decided to surprise me at work. Mike Wohlwend, you came in probably at my lowest point and you made me smile, cry and laugh all in the same moment. You are an amazing person and even better friend. Thanks for being there for me.

Lastly, to Vicky Sosa, whom I have coached in cross country and track for the past 5 years. I was at track practice last spring coaching my high school team and Vicky and a few friends were stretching and talking as I walked up to them. This was the season after COVID so we were still not doing much. They were talking about how they miss doing this and that and Vicky spoke up and said, "I miss the old Chad". This was not said in a bad way at all. It did, however, hit me like a ton of bricks. I was a broken, battered person with a torn up knee. A person that was very discouraged, emotional and super depressed because I wasn't getting any better. In an instant I made a split decision to change my attitude and see the light at the end of the tunnel instead of what has happened. In that instant I decided to look at a brighter future, to see what was possible if I did what I needed to do to get better. Vicky, by saying that to me you literally saved my life in that one instant. Thanks for being honest with me and speaking up. You are and always will be my savior!

Finally, I cannot leave out my family. I have taken away vital time with you to write this book. Although I tried not to work on the book during family time, I know at times I did and I'm sorry. Thank you for allowing me to push through and get this done. I not only write this book for anyone in the world that I can help but also for you, my family. This book will by no means help support our family financially, and that was not its purpose, but it was created to help inspire you to do and become something you didn't think you could before, and to help my business become more successful which in turn helps you... my family. We are in this together. Thank you and I love you!

SOURCE MATERIAL

CHAPTER 1

- Shaping Concepts is located in Point Pleasant, South Carolina

CHAPTER 3

- Thomas Worthington High School is located in Worthington, Ohio

CHAPTER 4

- Bob Willey is the Head Track & Field Coach at the University of Rio Grande in Rio Grande, Ohio
- Coach Gallagher was the Head Track and Field Coach at Ashland University in Ashland, Ohio
- Book—Iron Heart by Brian Boyle, 2009, 2011 Skyhorse Publishing
- Book—Unthinkable by Scott Rigsby, 2009, Tyndale House Publishers
- Book—Can't Hurt Me by David Goggins, 2018, Lioncrest Publishing

- Scott Kathmann is a Physical Therapist at Elite Physical Therapy in Bluffton, South Carolina

CHAPTER 5

- Song—The Climb by Mylie Cyrus, https://www.youtube.com/watch?v=NG2zyeVRcbs
- Jonathan Riddle is a Pastor at The Church of the Cross in Bluffton, South Carolina

CHAPTER 6

- "When you fail, make sure you fall on your back…" was said by motivation speaker, Les Brown, https://www.youtube.com/watch?v=NQ4en7o8B-g&t=337s 3:56 into the video

CHAPTER 8

- "If you died today, what would be written on your Tombstone?" was coined by Todd Durkin, the owner at Fitness Quest 10 in San Diego, California, https://www.facebook.com/watch/?v=889542888282630

CHAPTER 10

- How to block your time was in the book Get Your Mind Right by Todd Durkin, Baker Books 2020
- Purewave massage gun is at https://www.padousa.com

- Powerdot Tens Unit is at https://www.powerdot.com

CHAPTER 11

- Katherine Rosenblum is the Head Track Coach at May River High School in Bluffton, South Carolina
- Jermaine Bigham is the Head Girls Basketball Coach at May River High School in Bluffton, South Carolina
- Book-Coming Back Stronger, by Drew Brees, 2015 Tyndale House Publishers

CHAPTER 13

- "You play to win the game" was said by Herm Edwards, https://www.youtube.com/watch?v=AK7fEjrqabg

CHAPTER 15

- Mitch Brown is the owner of Boat Float in Bluffton, South Carolina

CHAPTER 18

- Tim Waz is the owner of Grounded Running in Beaufort, South Carolina
- Zeal is a product of Zurvita https://zurvita.com
- Cannonfit is owned by Chad Cannon, located in Bluffton, South Carolina www.cannonfit.com

- Benefits of drinking water is from Healthline Medically reviewed by Jillian Kabala,-Nutrition — Written by Joe Leech, MS — Updated on June 30, 2020 https://www.healthline.com/nutrition/7-health-benefits-of-water
- The importance of sleep is from Healthline Medically reviewed by Atli Arnason— Written by Joe Leech, MS on February 24, 2020 https://www.healthline.com/nutrition/10-reasons-wh y-good-sleep-is-important

CHAPTER 19

- Bob Willey, The University of Rio Grande
- Make time to workout on Sundays was said by Dwayne "the Rock" Johnson https://www.menshealth.com/fitness/a36873853/dwayne-johnson-the-rock-sunday-workout-gym

CHAPTER 20

- Book—Toughness by Jay Bilas, 2014 Published by the Penguin Group
- The "what's next" mentality was coined by Mike Krzyzewski

CHAPTER 21

- Benefits of eating protein, Healthline 10 reasons to eat more protein, Written by Kris Gunnars, BSc — Updated on March 8, 2019 https://www.healthline.com/nutrition/10-reasons-to-ea t-more-protein

- Benefits of eating complex carbohydrates, Healthline Simple carbohydrates vs. complex carbohydrates, Medically reviewed by Katherine Marengo, Nutrition — Written by Kristeen Cherney — Updated on August 19, 2020 https://www.healthline.com/health/food-nutrition/simple-carbohydrates-complex-carbohydrates
- Benefits of eating fruits and vegetables, Fruits and Vegetables, Harvard, https://www.hsph.harvard.edu/nutritionsource/what-should-you-eat/vegetables-and-fruits/
- Boosting the metabolism, 10 ways to boost your Metabolism, WebMD, Reviewed by Kathleen M. Zelman on September 12, 2019, https://www.webmd.com/diet/ss/slideshow-boost-your-metabolism
- Calorie counter at https://www.calculator.net/calorie-calculator.html

CHAPTER 22

- 5 fundamental movements are from https://cathe.com/5-movement-patterns-master-greater-functional-strength
- Mobility, what is mobility training & why it should become part of your routine?28th April 2021 https://evofitness.ch/mobility-training/
- Force production, muscle force production and transmission, https://us.humankinetics.com/blogs/excerpt/muscle-force-production-and-transmission
- Metabolic conditioning, Metabolic conditioning; the key to better performance, https://www.mensjournal.com/health-fitness/metabolic-conditioning-the-key-to-better-performance

CHAPTER 28

- Body starts breaking down... When Does Your Body Start to Age? 1800 health Simplifying healthcare. https://1800health. com/general/statistics/when-does-your-body-start-to-age/

CHAPTER 29

- Calm App is at www.calm.com

CHAPTER 31

- "How to use essential oils for the Flu" Healthline April 1, 2019, Medically reviewed by Debra Rose Wilson, — Written by Jennifer Purdie — Updated on April 1, 2019, https://www. healthline.com/health/cold-flu/essential-oils-for-flu
- "18 essential oils you can use to boost your energy" Healthline August 20, 2019, Medically reviewed by Debra Rose Wilson — Written by Scott Frothingham on August 20, 2019, https:// www.healthline.com/health/essential-oils-for-energy

CHAPTER 32

- Abby Rhoades is a Message Therapist at CannonFit in Bluffton, South Carolina
- Reasons why massage is so important is by Abby Rhoades on the Push-ups and Pizza Podcast by Chad Cannon and Sandy Benson, https://anchor.fm/chad-cannon/episodes/ The-benefits-of-different-types-of-Massage-evh57v

- Benefits of foam rolling, Medically reviewed by Daniel Bubnis, Fitness — Written by Jane Chertoff on April 11, 2019, https://www.healthline.com/health/foam-roller-benefits#muscle-pain
- Scott Kathmann is a Physical Therapist at Elite Physical Therapy in Bluffton, South Carolina
- Purewave by Pado, https://www.padousa.com

CHAPTER 34

- Treating pain with heat and cold, Medically reviewed by Judith Marcin — Written by Ana Gotter — Updated on March 7, 2019, https://www.healthline.com/health/chronic-pain/treating-pain-with-heat-and-cold
- Benefits of Cryotherapy, Medically reviewed by Debra Rose Wilson — Written by Ana Gotter — Updated on March 2, 2020, https://www.healthline.com/health/cryotherapy-benefits

CHAPTER 35

- Benefits of Red light therapy, Healthline red light therapy March 5, 2020. Medically reviewed by Cynthia Cobb — Written by Jacquelyn Cafasso — Updated on March 5, 2020, https://www.healthline.com/health/red-light-therapy
- What is red light therapy? WebMD October 13, 2019, By Camilla Noe Pagan, Medically Reviewed by Melinda Ratini, on October 13, 2019, https://www.webmd.com/skin-problems-and-treatments/red-light-therapy
- Platinum LED therapy lights for red light therapy, http.www.platinumtherapylights.com

CHAPTER 36

- Under Armour Recovery (TM) https://www.underarmour.com/en-us/search?q=recovery&search-button=&lang=en_US
- SleepMaster Sleep Mask http://www.sleepmaster.us

CHAPTER 39

- Jar of Awesome is in Book—Tools of Titans by Tim Ferris pages 570, 571

CHAPTER 40

- Song—Walking the Wire by Imagine Dragons, https://www.youtube.com/watch?v=1nv9br7P7g0

CHAPTER 42

- Sidney Mcloughlin, Faith, https://www.klove.com/news/faith/giving-credit-to-god-sydney-mclaughlin-representing-america-at-the-olympics-24545

FINAL THOUGHTS

- Mantras by Mona Huff

PEOPLE MENTIONED THROUGHOUT THE BOOK

CHAPTER 1

- Tracey Cannon, Madeline Cannon, Calem Cannon and Emerson Cannon, my family
- Mackenzee Vance, CannonFit client and collegiate soccer player UCLA

CHAPTER 3

- Coach Gary Smith, Cross Country & Track Coach at Thomas Worthington High School, Worthington, Ohio

CHAPTER 4

- Coach Bob Wiley, Cross Country & Track Coach at the University of Rio Grande, Rio Grande, Ohio (also in Chapter 18, 19)
- Coach Gallagher, Track Coach at Ashland University, Ashland, Ohio

- Brian Boyle, Book "Iron Heart"
- Scott Rigsby, Book "Unthinkable"
- Scott Kathmann, Elite Physical Therapy (also in Chapter 32)
- David Goggins, Book "Can't Hurt Me"

CHAPTER 5

- Pastor Jonathan Riddle, Church of the Cross—Miley Cyrus, Song "The Climb"

CHAPTER 6

- Les Brown, Motivational Speaker

CHAPTER 7

- Rod and Lynnea Imhoff, friends forever

CHAPTER 8,10

- Todd Durkin, Owner/Coach of Fitness Quest 10

CHAPTER 10

- Katherine Rosenblum, Head Cross Country & Track coach at May River High School, Bluffton, South Carolina
- Jermaine Bigham, Head Varsity Girls

- Basketball Coach at May River High School, Bluffton, South Carolina

CHAPTER 11

- Drew Brees, NFL Quarterback

CHAPTER 12

- Coach Jeff McGarvey, Dublin Middle School
- Track Coach Jeff McCutchen, middle school and high school friend and teammate

CHAPTER 13

- Herm Edwards, Former NFL Head Coach

CHAPTER 15

- Mitch Brown, Owner of Boat Floats and dear friend

CHAPTER 18

- Tim Waz, Owner of Grounded Running
- Coach Bob Wiley, Cross Country & Track
- Coach at the University of Rio Grande, Rio Grande, Ohio

CHAPTER 19

- Coach Bob Wiley, Cross Country & Track Coach at the University of Rio Grande, Rio Grande, Ohio
- Dwayne "The Rock" Johnson, Actor

CHAPTER 20

- Coach Mike Krzyzewski, Head Men's Basketball Coach at Duke University, Durham, North Carolina

CHAPTER 32

- Abby Rhoades, Massage Therapist, Massage Life, at CannonFit.
- Scott Kathmann, Physical Therapist, Elite Physical Therapy

CHAPTER 39

- Tim Ferriss, Book "Tools Of Titans"

CHAPTER 40

- Imagine Dragons, Song "Walking The Wire"

CHAPTER 42

- Sidney Mcloughlin, 2x Olympian and world record holder 400 meter hurdles

FINAL THOUGHTS

- Mona Huff, CannonFit client and friend

FINDING YOUR *Wooooo!*

WORKBOOK

SUCCEEDING AT YOUR HEALTH & FITNESS GOALS

GETTING YOUR BODY BACK THE CANNONFIT WAY

BY
CHAD CANNON

CONNECT WITH CHAD

CANNONFIT.COM

TUNE IN TO CHAD'S
PODCAST

Coach Chad Cannon & Sandy Benson

The Push-Ups & Pizza Podcast is designed to help create motivation and inspiration, as well as educated about structure for better fitness. This podcast is from two points of views; a coach and a client. The podcast is for anyone who seeks higher success in mind, body and soul.

Available on Anchor and Spotify

CPSIA information can be obtained
at www.ICGtesting.com
Printed in the USA
LVHW051347050122
707923LV00016B/1062